# FI

## and

# HEALING

# THROUGH THE BIBLE

Roy Lawrence spent 38 years in parish ministry, during which time he demonstrated how the local church can be an effective centre for the practice of Christian healing. The parish of Prenton, Birkenhead, where he was vicar for 21 years, became a prototype for those wishing to develop this ministry. Since retiring from parish ministry he has become Honorary Consultant of the Acorn Healing Trust to the Churches' Advisers in Healing. He is married to Eira, a chartered physiotherapist. They have two sons and three grandchildren.

*In grateful memory
of the Reverend George Bennett
and of Doctor Frank Lake
both of whom helped me
to find hope and healing through the Bible.*

# FINDING HOPE
## and
# HEALING
# THROUGH THE BIBLE

### Roy Lawrence

TRIANGLE

Published in Great Britain in 2000 by
Triangle
SPCK
Holy Trinity Church
Marylebone Road
London NW1 4DU

Bible extracts are from the Good News Bible, published by The Bible
Societies/HarperCollins Publishers Ltd UK © American Bible Society,
1966, 1971, 1976, 1992.

British Library Cataloguing-in-Publication Data

A catalogue record for this book is available from the British Library

ISBN 0–281–05352–9

Typeset by Pioneer Associates, Perthshire
Printed in Great Britain by
Omnia Books Ltd, Bishopbriggs, Glasgow

# Contents

*The stories in this book are all based on real events,
but in order to preserve anonymity
most of the names and some of the details have been
changed.*

# The Bible is a Book about Healing

'I read the Bible like a starving man eats bread,' writes the Korean pastor, Dr Paul Yonggi Cho. It is no surprise that he should say so. For it was as he read the Bible that he was healed of supposedly incurable tuberculosis.

In the coming pages my aim is to show that the Bible is primarily a book about healing – the healing of life at every level: body, mind and spirit, attitudes, emotions, relationships and lifestyles, healing for individuals and healing for society, healing within time and healing for eternity.

The Bible begins with 'the leaves of shame' in Genesis and ends with 'the leaves of healing' in Revelation. For this change of leaves to become a reality, God has embarked upon a mission to the human race. The Bible tells its story. The Old Testament tells how God has called a 'chosen people' and equipped them with gifts to help them understand and pursue their calling. The New Testament tells how out of this chosen people has come the 'Messiah', a Promised One, who has embodied God's healing purpose within his own life and work, and who has commissioned his followers to continue that work in the present and to look forward to its completion at the end of the age.

As we turn the pages of the Bible, we find that they constitute a folio of healing, full of insights, all of which have a power and life of their own. They lay a trail to the rediscovery of wholeness. All who have a mind to do so may follow it.

However, the Bible can seem an intimidating book. It is not easy to grasp as a whole. Its overall shape and purpose can elude us. This is perhaps because it is a 'library' rather than a single book. Nonetheless the 39 books of the Old Testament and the 27 books of the New Testament are not haphazard either in the themes they contain or the order in which they are arranged. The Bible has a real unity and structure, and it is all connected with God's will to bring healing to his damaged world and to the damaged people within it.

This is how I see its contents.

First there is a *Prologue* (Genesis 1—11), five dramas which, though they are set against the backcloth of the dawn of history, span the centuries in their relevance. For they are full of important truths about the nature of God, the nature of humankind, the purpose of creation and the enigma of evil.

*Section One* follows (from Genesis 12 to the book of Esther) and it tells the story of God's chosen people, the heights and the depths of their history, and the way in which they ranged between times of power and times of helplessness, between victory and defeat, between faith and faithlessness, between suffering and deliverance.*

*Section Two* consists of five books, dealing with some of life's major themes – Job with suffering, Psalms with worship, Proverbs with practical wisdom, Ecclesiastes with doubt, and the Song of Solomon with sexual love.

*Section Three* contains the writings of the Prophets (from Isaiah to Malachi). These were men who were well aware that God's purposes were far from complete, and yet saw his hand in history. In the light of this understanding they commented on the national and international events of their time. They also taught that there was more divine action to come and so they pointed ahead to the New Testament.

*Section Four* brings us to Jesus the Messiah, and his followers. Their story is told in the four Gospels and in the Acts of the Apostles.

*Section Five* deals with questions of practical Christianity. There are letters from St Paul and others (from the detailed doctrinal Epistle to the Romans to the brief warning note from Jude). The three opening chapters of Revelation also come into this section.

Finally there is an *Epilogue* (Revelation 4—22), a further drama for this and every age. In contrast to the Prologue, the backcloth is now that of the end of history as we know it. It considers the eventual intersection of time and eternity and affirms that in spite of the destructive power of evil, God's purpose must ultimately triumph.

There will be a more detailed overview of the Bible in the main part of this book, when I shall aim to share some of the ways in which Scripture has spoken to me personally about the healing purpose of God and has helped me both to receive that healing and to offer it to others. Then the Epilogue will contain some suggestions about ways in which you may discover the healing power of the Bible for yourself.

My hopes and prayers for myself and for you as we make this journey through Scripture together are that our healing Bible and the healing God for whom and of whom it speaks may both be increasingly known to us as living and personal realities.

In the words of the hymn by R. Hudson Pope:

> Make the Book live to me, O Lord,
> Show me Yourself within Your Word.

*For those interested in dates and details of Old Testament history – it was about 1900 BC when Abraham journeyed from his home in Iraq to Palestine. His family grew into the Israelite nation, which prospered initially but suffered slavery in Egypt from about 1700 to 1250. They returned to Palestine after wandering in the desert from 1250 to 1210. Then for 180 years they were led by a sequence of assorted leaders known in the Bible as 'judges'. This period was followed by 200 years of united monarchy (under Saul 1030–1010, David 1010–970, and Solomon 970–931). The united monarchy split into two divided kingdoms (under Rehoboam and his successors in the South and Jeroboam and his successors in the North). The Northern Kingdom, known as Israel, was conquered by Syria in 722 when its people were scattered throughout the world. The Southern Kingdom, known as Judah, was conquered by Babylon in 587/6 when the main part of the people went into exile. The exiles were allowed back to Jerusalem in 538, where they lived mostly under Persian rule till 333. (This was followed by a time of Greek rule till 166, Jewish rule till 63 and Roman rule up to and into New Testament times.)

# CHAPTER ONE

## *In the Beginning . . .*

### Read Genesis 1.1—2.4

'You really can't expect me to believe this rubbish,' said Gerald. 'Creation in seven days! Adam and Eve! The garden of Eden! A talking snake! Come off it!'

He was an intelligent man and liked to think of himself as having a scientific mind, and there are a dozen or so similar people who come into my mind, as I remember him. They would all have said much the same thing. They wrote off the Bible because they took the view that a book which seemed to them so untrue at a literal and scientific level could not be true in any way at all.

Oddly enough, none of them would have applied this principle to most of the other literature which they read. Elsewhere they would have had no difficulty in seeing that truth can be expressed in many ways – in poetry and parable, for instance. So when Robert Burns writes 'O, my Luve's like a red, red rose,' they would not be so literal as to ask, 'Where are her leaves and flowers and prickles?' Nor would they wipe out C. S. Lewis's Narnia stories on the grounds that you cannot locate Narnia on the globe and in any case a lion cannot talk.

There are in fact sometimes uncanny instances of scientific accuracy in Genesis (like the concept of life coming out of the waters), but to investigate Genesis on such a level is to miss its point, its purpose and its potential as a drama for our day.

So what do the early chapters of Genesis seek to say to us? Do they contain healing truths? And, if so, where and how can we find them?

## Creation versus chaos

In the first two verses of Genesis, Chapter 1, we are introduced to two contrasting forces. On the one hand there is a raging and chaotic watery waste. The Hebrew words which describe it are *tohu* and *bohu* – 'confusion' and 'emptiness'. On the other hand there is God in all his creative power.

Immediately Genesis presents us with the Bible's first fundamental healing concept: when the forces of chaos confront the power of the Creator, it is the Creator who prevails. It must be so because God is God.

This is a foundation belief of the Christian faith – and of many other world religions too. When we look around the world and feel overwhelmed by the chaos and destructiveness which engulf so many people and so many places, it is good to remember Genesis 1. Also in our own personal life, if we feel that things are falling apart, Genesis 1 has its own healing relevance here too. As a first exercise in finding healing in the Bible, you may like to pause at this point and say these words as an act of reflective prayer. 'Creation is stronger than chaos. For God is God. I can align my will with his will in quietness and confidence. I can rest in his strength and creativity.'

Gerald took exception to the presentation of creation as a seven-day sequence. He had not taken the trouble to find out that the Hebrew word for day, *yom*, does not have to mean 24 hours. We have a similar usage in English. If I say that life was different in my grandfather's day, I am using the word 'day' to denote the best part of a century, because he lived to the age of 98. If I look back to the 'day' of the dinosaur, then the word comes to mean something like a hundred million years!

But for now perhaps we may set aside this sort of issue. There are deeper and more therapeutic truths to consider in Genesis than the length of a *yom*. Here are four of them:

1   The first is the whole concept of creativity, which under-lies the early chapters of Genesis. You and I are not bits of flotsam and jetsam, thrown up accidentally by a universe which is itself an accident. Neither we nor our universe are haphazard. Both in us and around us there is creativity, design, purpose, mystery. So if you and I are ever tempted to write ourselves off as persons of slight value, Genesis reminds us that *God made us*, and that he is a skilled creator who does not make rubbish.

2   When God made this universe of which you and I are a part, he took pleasure in it. Again and again we read in Genesis 1 that God 'was pleased' with creation, that it was 'very good' in his sight. God not only made us. *God values us*. We are precious to him. Self-contempt is not humility but blasphemy. Of course we have gone wrong in all kinds of ways. But the basic material in us is good. According to the traditional translation of Psalm 139.14, you and I are 'fearfully and wonderfully made'. God will never consign us to a cosmic scrapheap and we must never do so either.

3   If we should ever feel insignificant tiny creatures in a vast universe, here is another healing concept from Genesis 1: God values little things as well as big things. We are obsessed by size. God is not. *God is concerned about all creatures great and small* – the grass as well as the galaxies.

4 As far as the human race is concerned, even though in this book we shall not preoccupy ourselves with the order of the days in Genesis 1, it must be significant that the creation of humankind comes as a climax in the order of events. It must also be significant that Genesis makes it clear that as humans we have a special and distinctive role. There is something quite unique which we are called to do and to be. In other words *God wants us*.

Only a few days before I wrote these words I was talking to Walter, a man with a painfully low sense of self-esteem, and I found myself suggesting that it could be therapeutic for him if he made a point of saying at the beginning and end of every day, 'God made me, God values me, God wants me.' He has just been on the phone to say that these Genesis concepts are already making a healing difference to him.

And the more we consider just what it is that God wants us for, the more amazing our purpose and destiny seems to be. According to Genesis 1, God made humankind to 'have power' (verse 26), to 'bring the earth under control' (verse 28), and even 'to be like himself' (verse 27)! For you and I not only contain ingredients which we share with the animal, vegetable and mineral worlds. We are also spiritual beings, mysteriously made in the image of God. There is more to us than our biochemical ingredients, and in the name of the God whose image we bear we must treasure each other and treasure ourselves.

## The Genesis of you and me

There we could end this Bible study, but before we do so here is a further thought. It is a strange one, and I owe it to Origen, a theologian of the early Church, who lived from about AD 185 to about 254, and who was famed (and sometimes defamed) for his speculative thinking. He wrote, 'Understand, you have within you, upon a small scale, a second universe.'

In other words the universe is a macrocosm which contains many a microcosm. Each microcosm is a mini-universe in its own right, and these mini-universes include you and me. One of the reasons why the Genesis creation stories are personally relevant to us is that our time on earth is a creative process in its own right. 'Call the world, if you please, the vale of soul-making,' wrote John Keats. The beginning of Genesis can perhaps be regarded as a parable which can help us to understand just what is the nature of the soul that you and I are in the process of becoming and how we can best move forwards in the creation process.

Like Genesis we have a tendency to divide this process into seven stages. In my earlier book *Christ with Us* I find that, without planning to do so, I have divided life into seven phases – childhood, adolescence, the early adult years, the prime of life, the years when we are past our prime but still at work, the retirement years and finally the experience of dying. Shakespeare also divides life into 'seven ages' in *As You Like It*. His picture is notably more jaundiced than mine, since it is no part of his purpose to consider the healing influence of Jesus. So he describes the ages of man as those of the mewling infant, the whining schoolboy, the sighing lover, the swearing soldier, the round-bellied justice, the slippered pantaloon and finally the descent into second childhood and oblivion.

The question which we may find ourselves asking in the light of our present Bible study is whether the seven days of Genesis hold any hints for us in our own sevenfold pattern of life development. It is a question which I believe can help us discover further healing truths, as we probe this remarkable passage of Scripture. Here are four of them.

1    It is worth noting that if we view Genesis 1 as a parable of our own life development, its standpoint is anti-ageist. In the sequence of the 'days' there is always a reason to look forward. The movement is always upwards and onwards. By contrast, our conventional assumption is 'Shakespearian' in its pessimism. We see life as rapidly going into decline, ebbing away as the years go by. I shudder to remember that when I was a student I presumptuously asked a woman in her fifties whether she was troubled by the passage of the years. Like the Christian she was, she answered with patience and courtesy, and her reply has remained with me over the years. She said, 'If you take Christianity seriously, life actually gets better. Each day with Jesus takes you further than the day before. The aging of your body is a very small price to pay.' She had a Genesis perspective and it clearly served her well.

2    In the first five days of creation in Genesis 1 the emphasis is on the material and not on the spiritual. The same is often true in human life. In our earlier years we join body-building clubs, work at making money and try to get on in the world. But if we let ourselves be fixated at this point, if we become permanently circumscribed by the material and physical, our development as human beings will be incomplete.

3    Completion does not come in Genesis till the concept of spirituality has been introduced. There is more to creation than its animal, vegetable and mineral facets. It is God's purpose mysteriously to share something of himself, and though we can discover our spiritual potential at any age, the fact that in Genesis it happens on the sixth day is quite an encouragement to those who have arrived at stage six on the human journey. It reminds us that the retirement years provide a unique opportunity

for discovering who we are meant to be and what we are meant to become.

4   And what of the final stage? In Genesis there are six active stages and then one of rest. It is the same with life – and virtually all of us fear the seventh stage. Even those who have no fear of death often fear death's waiting room. Shakespeare clearly abhorred it and described it as a time 'sans teeth, sans eyes, sans taste, sans everything'. But by contrast in Genesis the seventh phase is a time of blessing. 'God,' we are told, 'blessed the seventh day and set it apart as special.'

So here is a surprising message of hope and healing. I know from pastoral experience that it can be true. Those who find themselves in life's departure lounge are not necessarily unhappy. Most activities may have stopped, but not the flow of blessings. I think of Nancy who sent for me just hours before she died. She said, 'I just wanted to tell you how blessed I feel.' Or there was Felicity who was terrified of death but came to our vicarage after watching her father die. 'He was radiant,' she said. 'I can never be afraid of death again.' Or there was my own grandmother. Her husband and her children were gathered round her deathbed, urging her to fight for life, to hold on, to come back to them. But her eyes were focused on something the rest of them could not see. 'Don't hold me back, my dears,' she said. 'I want to go. It's all so lovely.' The seven stages of her creation had run their course, but she had no doubt that this had brought her not to an end but to a new beginning. She found death a healing, an experience of birth (which of course is just what the word genesis means).

However, what if you feel that the optimism of this chapter does not correspond with real life? Genesis may claim that at the end of the seven days of creation everything was 'very good'. But as you look at the world around you, things seem far from being 'very good'. What about the immorality and violence which we see on the TV? What about the obvious flaws in society? What about the pain and grief which are so evident in the lives of people around us – and maybe in our own? Is the Bible blind to the fact that, whatever the Creator's original intention may have been, the world has gone horrendously wrong? Not at all. That is why Genesis 1 is followed by Genesis 2 and 3. And that is why it is now time for us to bring on the talking snake.

CHAPTER TWO

# Catastrophe in a Garden

## Read Genesis 2.4b—3.24

Halfway through the fourth verse of Genesis 2, there is a
marked change of perspective and style. Scholars tell us that
it happens because at this point we move from material
preserved by priests for use in the Temple to folk tales
passed on by parents and grandparents to their children.

The lofty cosmic concerns of Genesis 1 give way to a more
homely atmosphere. The camera zooms in from panning the
galaxies and we find ourselves in a garden on earth, meeting
a man called Adam.

Once again we are offered not just a legend from the
dusty past but a drama of present-day relevance. One of
the clues that this is so lies in the names that are used. It is
rather like John Bunyan's *Pilgrim's Progress*, where the
names have meaning, as in the case of Christian, Faithful,
Greatheart, Giant Despair, the Slough of Despond, and so
on. 'Adam' is the Hebrew for 'mankind'. 'Eden' is the
Hebrew for 'delight'. So here is a story to explain in picture
language how humankind could have lived in a garden of
delight, had we not misused our free will and in the process
brought deep trouble upon ourselves.

Genesis tells of the provision of a companion for Adam.
Her name, 'Eve', means 'life', because it was God's will for
life to flow from their union and because they themselves

could have discovered a new fullness of life as together they explored their relationship. Adam was meant to be one with Eve and he recognized this by his initial response to her. 'Here is one of my own kind – bone taken from my bone and flesh from my flesh' (Genesis 2.23).

'Oneness' is a key word in understanding Genesis and in understanding what it means to be fully human. We are meant to accept oneness with each other and oneness with much more besides. It is all in Genesis 2.

## Paradise lost

The story tells how God breathed his own essence into Adam's nostrils to show that we are meant to be *one with the life of God* (verse 7). God set Adam in the Garden of Delight to show that we are meant to be *one with the joy of God* (verse 15). God brought all the animals and birds to Adam to be named to show that we are meant to be *one with creation* (verse 19). God made the gift of Eve to Adam and Adam to Eve to show that we are meant to be *one with each other* (verse 23). And we are told that neither Adam nor Eve were ashamed of their nakedness. For we are meant to be *one with our inner selves* (verse 25).

But what a contrast when we turn from Genesis 2 to Genesis 3! Here we find Adam and Eve covering their nakedness. They have lost their inner integrity. They have become *separated from themselves* (verse 7). They hide from their Creator, for they have become *separated from God* (verse 8). We find Adam blaming Eve for it all, for they have become *separated from each other* (verse 12). They no longer know how to co-operate with or enjoy the good earth, for they are *separated from creation* (verse 17). As the story ends they are driven out of the Garden of Eden, *separated from joy and from all that is best in life* (verses 23–24).

So what happened to cause such a total and catastrophic change? Superficially it happened because Adam and Eve took and tasted fruit from a forbidden tree. But there has to be more to it than a simple case of fruit-stealing.

My first vicarage had an orchard as part of its garden but the apples rarely found their way into our kitchen. They were more likely to be found in the pockets and stomachs of the village children. Stealing fruit was almost a parish sport. The locals called it 'scrumping' and had a good laugh at it, as long as it was not their own fruit that was vanishing.

Those of us who suffered from scrumpers perhaps did not find it quite so easy to see the funny side of it. My wife, Eira, makes a lovely apple pie, given the right ingredients, and I have to admit that I had less than kindly thoughts towards those responsible for denuding our apple trees. However, never for a moment would I have wished to cast a total blight upon their lives for ever and upon the lives of their children after them, which is what happened to Adam and Eve. Their banishment from the Garden of Delight and the centuries of trouble that followed for them and their descendents would be totally inappropriate if we were to take this story completely at a literal level. We have to go beneath the surface and penetrate the symbolism.

So what do we make of this tale of two mysterious trees and a sinister talking snake?

First we must take note that there are *two* trees of special symbolism and not just one at the heart of the garden. We are introduced to them both in Genesis 2.9. In most translations one is called 'the tree of life' and the other is called 'the tree of the knowledge of good and evil'.

There is no restriction placed on access to the tree of life. Like most of the trees in the garden it was freely available and Adam and Eve were welcome to take its fruit. God wanted them and wants us to enjoy the fullness of life.

However, the second tree was forbidden to them. It was not yet time for Adam and Eve to experience the difference between good and evil, and in the story initially they seemed content to have it so. But then the talking snake reared its head. The book of Revelation speaks of 'that old serpent, called the Devil' (Revelation 12.9, AV, and see 20.2). So perhaps it is not fanciful to see this as the first appearance of Satan in the pages of Scripture.

The methodology and the content of the serpent's temptation are both significant, because both are encountered in the world today and you and I are just as susceptible to them as Adam and Eve were. The methodology consisted of a bombardment with half-truths. Just listen to the snake in action in this paraphrase of the dialogue with Eve in Genesis 3.1–6:

Snake    What sort of a God would put you into an orchard and tell you that you can't eat any of the fruit?

Eve      It isn't like that. We can eat any of the fruit except that of just one tree, the one that gives knowledge of good and evil. God says the fruit from that tree would be deadly for us.

Snake    He wants to keep it for himself, that's why. God knows about good and evil, for sure, and it doesn't do him any harm. He just wants to keep you under his thumb! But why shouldn't you know what he knows? Go on. Be like God! Find out about good and evil. Try *everything*.

Eve      Well, it does look tempting. And it would be wonderful to know what God knows. And I'm sure that if I taste it, Adam will want to try it too . . .

I wonder how many half-truths you can identify here. Some of them are in full view. Some are merely implied and are all the more dangerous for that. And I wonder if you can spot the actual core of the temptation here. It has nothing to do with an apple-core! It is contained in three words – *Be like God*. Most modern translations contain precisely those words. Adam and Eve were being offered a theological do-it-yourself kit or, even worse, a be-it-yourself kit. They were being tempted to take God from the centre of life and substitute self there instead. They fell for it. And so do we.

Self-centredness is the basic sin, the basic folly, which has characterized human history for centuries. We have talked peace, but made war. We have been more interested in our own wealth and status and power than in the rights and needs of others. And what we have practised as a species we have embodied as individuals. You and I find it all too easy to centre our thoughts upon ourselves and to put our own interests first, to 'look after number one', as we say revealingly. For self and not God has become 'number one'. It is a deadly way of looking at life. Events have shown that it was God and not the serpent who spoke the truth. Paradoxically self-centredness goes with self-damage and ultimately, unless we can find help, it will lead to self-destruction.

In Genesis 2 and 3, when Adam and Eve fall for the temptation to treat self as their god, they become strangers to peace and joy. They are driven out of the Garden of Delight, and though the fruit of the tree of life could have been theirs, they find that this is no longer so. Their access to it is now barred by 'cherubim and a flaming sword flashing back and forth' (Genesis 3.24, NIV). So this is a story with a very unhappy ending.

Fortunately the whole story is not yet over. God is still God. As we saw in Genesis 1, he values his creation. Though we turn our backs upon him, he does not turn his back upon us. He has not abandoned humankind, even though we have flouted his law and become a flawed and fallen species. He has a plan, a policy, a gospel, and the story of the Bible does not end till the fruit of the tree of life is once again made available (Revelation 22.2). For God's will is for our reclamation and our healing.

Moreover, though the saga of the Garden of Eden ends in disaster, yet even in this unlikely context there are healing truths to be discerned, and it is important to make them our own before moving on. Here are four of them.

## What can we learn from the story of Eden?

First, it is worth reiterating the positivity of God's attitude towards us. Behind the apparent negativity of God's command that Adam and Eve should not eat the deadly fruit of the tree of the knowledge of good and evil was his positive desire that they should live, grow and be whole. The tree of life was originally freely available to them. When Jesus said of his disciples, 'I have come that they may have life, and have it to the full' (John 10.10, NIV), he was totally in accord with the mind and intent of the God of Genesis. *We* need to be on our guard against the serpent's half-truths. They are still circulating widely. They concentrate on the negative elements in God's laws and totally ignore the positive purpose behind them. The devil would, of course, prefer us not to believe in God at all, but if we will not buy the concept of a totally godless universe, then he offers us a picture of a negative God, a spoilsport God, a God with a crab-apple face, a God whose favourite phrase is 'thou shalt not', whereas by contrast he himself dons a winking, smirking mask which conceals the destructiveness lying behind it. His object is to stop us actually thinking. For once we start to see more than half-truths, it will be self evident that if God exists he *must* be actively pro-life. Otherwise he would never have created it in the first place.

Second, fullness of life does *not* mean trying everything. Though this is a popular notion in contemporary society, it is self-evidently wrong. There are many activities which expand us and do us good. They make for life and liberty and true happiness. But others are just the opposite and if we are concerned to experience life at its fullest and best we will avoid them.

My mind goes back to someone who learned this the hard way. Let's call her 'Polly'. Her story comes from my earliest days in the ministry, but it has a curiously modern ring. Polly became bored with her church youth club. She thought its activities were tame and restrictive and told her vicar, whom I knew well, that he and his club were a waste of time. 'I'm going to see life,' she said, as she walked out. After that for a long time he saw her only if he happened to catch a glimpse of her flashing past in the sports car of her latest man. There were a lot of them. She was pretty. She was popular. She was game for anything. Her aim was to have a good time. Her motto was 'try everything'.

Years later when her vicar was visiting the local hospital, unexpectedly he found himself at the foot of a bed in which the patient was Polly. Seeing her was a surprise, but the way she looked was a greater one. Polly's lifestyle had landed her with a sexual disease and it was a bad one. It had taken her looks and her health. She looked ravaged and wretched.

'Do you remember,' she asked him, 'how I told you I was going to see life?' Before he could answer, she went on, 'Well, I've seen it. And I wish to God I hadn't.'

The trouble with trying everything is that we live in a world of cause and effect and everything has its consequence. The problem is that all too often we find this out the hard way, when perhaps excessive nicotine has messed up our lungs, or excessive alcohol has messed up our liver, when promiscuity has led to disease, or drugs have led to

addiction. The 'try everything' policy can be just as dangerous for us as it was for Adam and Eve.

Third, the vital thing is that we should know our goals. If
we don't stand for something we will fall for anything. And
it is important that they should be truly ours, chosen with
intelligence and care; not goals that have been foisted on us
by peer pressure or media manipulation or any other vari-
ant of the serpent in the garden. Of course we all need help
in goal-selection. But it makes sense to be careful where we
go for it.

If Genesis is right, the best goals are those which will
help us become one with the life and the joy of God, one
with creation, one with our fellow humans and one with our
inner selves. If a goal has the opposite effect and separates
us from God and our fellow humans and our own inner
integrity, if it militates against life and joy and makes us
strangers within creation, then we should shun it, just as we
would shun a foul disease.

Fourth, above all if we are concerned about wholeness at
every level of our being, we need to accept the Genesis
insight that there is *no substitute for God at the centre of
life*. This is the heart of the message not only of Genesis 2
and 3 but of the Bible as a whole. Providing God exists, then
to accept him as the key to and core of our own being makes
very good sense. For by doing so it follows logically that we
will have chosen a strong centre, a safe centre and a centre
which will unite us. If on the other hand we fall for the serpent's temptation and opt to try to make life revolve around
self, we will inevitably find ourselves with a weak centre, an
unsafe centre, and a centre which will cause division at every
level of life.

In other words – to put Genesis 2 and 3 in a nutshell – we
shall never get back to the garden until we get back to God.

## CHAPTER THREE

# *Three More Dramas for Our Day*

**Read**  **Genesis 4.1–24**
  **Genesis 6.1—9.17**
  **Genesis 11.1–9**
  **Genesis 12.1–3**

By the time our tour of Scripture brings us to Genesis 12, we shall have come to the dawn of the history of the nation of Israel, a nation called – not altogether willingly – to become God's chosen people and to implement God's healing purposes within this damaged world. But before we come to Genesis 12, the Bible offers us three more parables from prehistory, ancient folk tales from the distant past, which for all their antiquity still speak directly to us here and now. The first is a tale of bad blood between brothers.

## Cain and Abel

At first sight the story of Cain and Abel can seem just an example of the way in which sibling rivalry can survive into adult life with very ugly consequences. But there is more here than meets the eye. Coming as it does straight after the story of the Garden of Eden, perhaps its main purpose is to remind us that Adam and Eve not only damaged themselves when they disobeyed God but that their children and children's children were affected too.

We may think that the third commandment sounds barbaric, when it speaks of the sins of the fathers being visited upon subsequent generations (Exodus 20.5), but at a practical level it is precisely what we see happening in life. You and I have not only the capacity to exercise a 'horizontal' influence by helping or hurting people in our own day and age but we can have a 'vertical' impact too. We influence those who come after us – for good or ill.

We do this both by the way in which we condition our children and also by the hereditary equipment with which we endow them in body, mind and spirit. Cedric comes into my mind, an irascible senior clergyman, who confided in me that he found himself unable to resist behaving with the same bad temper which he used to find so trying when displayed by his father. Or more seriously, I find myself thinking of Janine who was born with congenital syphilis. In her case I am pleased to be able to tell you that this condition disappeared after she received the ministry of Christian healing and she has been clear of it for many years now. But unless there is a powerful intervention, it is normal human experience that we are deeply affected by the choices our parents made and the lives they lived.

So the story of Cain and Abel is a warning. When Adam and Eve elected to put their own selfish personal whims before the will of God, they opened a Pandora's box crammed full of evils. Generations later their descendants were still grubbing about in it. In Cain we see selfish anger escalate into murderous rage. He murders his brother Abel and then tries to conceal the fact within a web of deceit. Later on in the family history Cain's sins are replicated and increased by a descendant called Lamech, who both committed murder and gloried in it (Genesis 4.23), rather like a terrorist boasting about those he has killed or maimed, or a sexual psychopath taking pleasure in the damage he has done to his victims.

How can such a story possibly have any sort of healing impact on us? First it may make us less judgemental when we consider our children and children's children. If we have trouble with them, what's new? Adam and Eve had the same trouble, but it stemmed from their own wrong choices, their own wrong behaviour. It was an inheritance.

So if we find ourselves complaining about declining standards in those who come after us, a moment of thought will probably show us that we ourselves have contributed to the decline. When I was a boy, society was in the process of turning away from religion. It was becoming fashionable to stay away from the churches and to denounce dogmas. The generally held notion was that you could behave like a Christian without believing in Christian doctrine. In vain the religious leaders of the day told us that if we abandoned Christian belief then Christian behaviour would go too, but events proved them right. What you believe affects what you do and what sort of person you become. Many of the seeds which are growing in society today as we move into a new millennium were sown half a century earlier.

And if the Cain and Abel story reduces our tendency to judgementalism, it might just also increase our sense of responsibility for the future. As Ramases says to his father, Seti, in Christopher Fry's play *The Firstborn*, 'It's you who invite the future, but it's I who have to entertain it, remember that.' Cain and Abel and Lamech and the rest were entertaining the future invited by Adam and Eve. You and I could perhaps have a healing effect on the future, if we upgrade our sense of responsibility for it. But if we don't, then we won't.

One of my least favourite characters in the Bible is

Hezekiah. When the prophet Isaiah tells him that his own mistakes will result in suffering and exile for future generations of his people, he is quite smug about it. In the words of 2 Kings 20.19, 'King Hezekiah understood this to mean that there would be peace and security during his lifetime, so he replied, "The message you have given me from the Lord is good."' His motto is clearly *Après moi le déluge*. (Let the flood come – provided it's after my time!) We need to make sure that it is not our own. But, speaking of floods, it is time to move on now to Genesis 6, 7, 8 and 9.

## The flood

The story of the flood is one which has intrigued many writers. Often they have speculated whether it could have historical origins or not. Certainly there were catastrophic floods in the ancient world. For example, there is archeological evidence of a flood in Mesopotamia. Babylonian folklore is full of it. But on the other hand the biblical story seems to refer to the whole world (see Genesis 6.17) and that cannot be supported by archeology. There is, for instance, no evidence, so far as I know, of such a flood in Australia.

But as in the case of the other early chapters of Genesis, this sort of speculation is not particularly fruitful. If we have another drama for today in this story, then our main concern must be to understand what it is saying to us here and now.

In some ways this is an ecological parable. It makes the point that all forms of life on earth must sink or swim together and that for good or ill we humans have a responsibility which extends beyond merely human concerns. But my purpose here is to concentrate on the message which it brings as far as human life, health and survival are concerned. At first sight it is a message containing precious little comfort.

St Paul put his finger on the prime meaning of the flood

story when he wrote, 'The wages of sin is death' (Romans 6.23, NIV). It reminds us that there can be only one logical conclusion to Adam and Eve's disobedience and to the consequential corruption of the human race. If sin and God are incompatible, then our sins must separate us from God and in doing so separate us from life itself. So we are told, 'When the Lord saw how wicked everyone on earth was and how evil their thoughts were all the time, he was sorry that he had ever made them and put them on the earth' (Genesis 6.5–6). 'God said to Noah, "I have decided to put an end to all mankind. I will destroy them completely, because the world is full of their violent deeds"' (Genesis 6.13). 'I am going to send a flood on the earth to destroy every living being. Everything on earth will die' (Genesis 6.17).

The warning still applies. We are still at risk – perhaps not from a watery flood, but certainly from a flood of violence, a flood of disease, a nuclear flood, a flood of ecological disasters, which we ourselves have triggered.

It is worth pausing and registering the fact that if the Bible is a book about healing, there are going to be plenty of warnings in it. Just as the safety of our vehicles on the roads requires many warning signs, so it is with safety of our souls on the journey of life. And the safety of our bodies too.

For far too long we have ignored the warning signs of Scripture. They are there for our health, our wholeness, our happiness. When I was a student at Oxford, I went to hear a lecture by a visiting psychologist who said he was not really interested in the concept of sin. He wanted to teach people to avoid the things that made them unhappy. But then, almost as an afterthought, he added rather wryly, 'Mind you, the things which make people unhappy often coincide with what Christians call sins.' My own experience of many years in pastoral ministry has endorsed this judgement.

'The wages of sin is death.' A society which disobeys

God's laws is unlikely to be either happy or healthy. A species which does so has its finger on a self-destruct button. For our own good, both collectively and individually, it is high time to read the story of the flood again. It makes good sense to be aware of danger.

However, the story of the flood is not all doom and gloom. Alongside the warnings there are also symbols of hope. Two of them are the ark and the rainbow.

The ark built by Noah and his family represents the fact that, no matter how dire circumstances may be, men and women of faith can do a great deal more than wring their hands in helplessness. They can still build the equivalent of an ark.

There is an example not far from my own home. The churches of Wirral have worked together to provide a shelter in Birkenhead which ensures that no homeless person is compelled to bear the rigours of winter outdoors. It is actually called 'The Ark'. It may not overcome those factors in society which drive people to leave their homes and live on the streets, but it means that our local clergy can offer vagrants more than a kind word and a sandwich and many individuals have found a place of safety within it.

It is not even necessary to find the wood of Noah's ark or the bricks and mortar of the Birkenhead ark. Faith and love can themselves provide the material out of which an 'ark' is created. Ernest Gordon's book *Miracle on the River Kwai* offers a notable example. Right at the heart of the sadistic prison regime to which prisoners of war were subjected as they were forced to build the notorious bridge over the River Kwai during World War II, a group of Christians linked together in order to deepen and develop their faith. They created their own 'ark' and found within it a hope and healing which gave them strength to survive the unspeakable brutality of the life they had to endure.

So the ark is a symbol of hope. It speaks to individuals rather than to society as a whole. It is the Bible's way of reminding us that even if society is sinking fast, God will enable those who hold firmly to their faith not to sink with it. There is no shortage of examples – Richard Wurmbrand in a communist prison in Romania, Jackie Pullinger in Hong Kong, Mother Teresa in Calcutta and many more.

But God has a concern for society as a whole and not just for individuals. This is where the rainbow comes in. Though the wages of sin is death, yet the flood of destruction is not to have the last word in history. God is Creator and therefore Re-creator. It is his will to reclaim and restore our species. By placing a rainbow at the heart of the rain itself God notifies us that there are further and better things to come within his healing purpose. The rainbow, says God, is 'the sign of the promise which I am making to all living beings' (Genesis 9.17).

However, before the book of Genesis tells us about the beginnings of God's rescue plan, it has one more drama for today to run across the screen of Scripture.

## The Tower of Babel

Scattered around the ancient world there were ziggurats, pyramidal stepped towers, built of sun-dried bricks and faced with kiln-baked bricks. They looked a bit like overgrown American wedding cakes. Each layer was slightly smaller than the one immediately beneath it and they could rise to a great height. They were found mainly in Mesopotamia. The one that is best preserved is at Ur, the city from which Abraham came. These ziggurats seem to have provided the inspiration for the final story in the prehistory section of Genesis.

The theme of the story is that we shall never find an

answer to the human predicament and to the dangers which that predicament presents unless we trust God. Our own unaided efforts, no matter how clever they and we may seem, will end in chaos and disaster. The men of Babel think they can scale the heights of heaven by their own efforts. They start to build a super-ziggurat to prove it. But inevitably it all ends in discord, disarray and disaster.

I once wrote a little song to retell this story and show how it relates to us now. It was written for BBC Radio Manchester (now Greater Manchester Radio) and was sung as the station launched its first series of religious broadcasts.

There was a chorus: 'Words, words, words: the world is full of words: and everybody speaks, but no one listens.' And there were these three verses:

> I'll build the Tower of Babel,
> I'll build it to the sky,
> I know that I am able
> And I'll build it strong and high.
> All men shall be my minions
> And listen to my word.
> I'll trust in my opinions
> And I'll see that they are heard.
>
> Now this is not a fable
> Of ages long ago.
> Each decade has its Babel
> And the heaps of chaos grow.
> And international powers
> And neighbours side by side
> Still boast of making towers
> Built of hatred, greed and pride.
>
> God looks upon our Babel.
> He sees the sights of shame.

That's why into a stable
Once a little baby came.
And Jesus speaks with a quiet voice
Within this world of din.
So, Babel-builders, hush your noise.
It's time for hearing him!

Equipping us for 'hearing him' is the prime purpose of the Bible. But first it must introduce us to the founder of the race into which he was to be born.

## The Call of Abraham

In Genesis 12 we come to the dawn of the history of the people of Israel. It was round about 1900 BC when Abraham (or Abram, as he was originally called) became aware that God was calling him to found a family which would eventually grow into a nation. This was God's commission: 'Leave your country, your relatives, and your father's home, and go to a land that I am going to show you. I will give you many descendants, and they will become a great nation. I will bless you and make your name famous, so that you will be a blessing' (Genesis 12.1–2). He was not only to receive God's blessing but to be its channel for the whole world. 'Through you,' said God, 'I will bless all the nations' (Genesis 12.3).

As we continue on our journey through the Scriptures, we shall see that Abraham's descendants will receive six gifts as God's chosen people to enable them to receive and to channel God's healing power. These six gifts will be dealt with in the next four chapters, but for now, if we are to take just one thought from the life and call of Abraham, perhaps it should be this. Abraham was just one person, but one person can actually make a considerable difference to the history of the world! If you and I sometimes look at the immense problems of society, and if we find ourselves feeling helpless and inadequate, totally unable to make any contribution of significance – remember Abraham. He was just a single human being, but he was God's man. And it is a major theme of the Bible that there is no limit to what any one of us and God can do together.

# CHAPTER FOUR

# *The Gift of Experience*

**Read Exodus 3.2–10**
**Exodus 14.5–31**
**Numbers 21.4–9**

It seemed an impossible commission for one man and his descendants: 'Leave your country . . . become a great nation . . . through you I will bless all the nations.' But when God commands, he always empowers, and as the Old Testament continues its story we see that the people of Israel were entrusted with six gifts to enable them to be the people of God.

The first gift was that of Experience. As the pages of history were turned, again and again the Israelites were offered lessons by life itself. From day to day, year to year and century to century they found a tutor in the practicalities of experience.

The learning process was not pain-free for them. It never is. For we have to accept the lessons that life wishes to teach us as distinct from the lessons that we ourselves would prefer to learn. It does not come easily. In the case of the Israelites there were two main lessons. One was the positive principle that in one way or another God delivers those who put their trust in him, no matter how great the difficulties they face. The other was the negative principle that turning your back on God brings disaster.

## The Exodus

The supreme illustration of the positive principle in the experience of the Israelites was provided some six hundred years after the call of Abraham. Abraham had become the father of Isaac. Isaac became the father of Jacob and Jacob had children of his own. The Israelites were growing into an extended family group. The problems of their family life had a curiously modern ring. There were factions and feuds and inheritance disputes. Both poverty and prosperity brought their own distinctive difficulties. There was famine in part of the world then, just as there is now, and it was to escape from a famine area that the whole family moved to Egypt. Initially they were welcomed and well treated thanks to the influence of one of Jacob's sons, Joseph, who had risen to a position of prominence in that land. But then everything went wrong. When Jacob and Joseph died, the good days died with them, and the Israelites were reduced to slavery by the Egyptians.

Their ultimate escape, led by Moses, is an amazing story. It began when Moses had a strange encounter with God in the desert. 'The angel of the LORD appeared to him as a flame coming from the middle of a bush. Moses saw that the bush was on fire but that it was not burning up' (Exodus 3.2). Elsewhere I have written at greater length about the mystery of God's Shekinah-light, as recorded here and elsewhere in Scripture and sometimes still experienced today (Lawrence, 1999). At present all that needs to be said is that it totally changed Moses' life. As he stood barefoot before the bush, he was aware of a fourfold message from God. 'I have seen how cruelly my people are being treated.' 'I have heard them cry out.' 'I have come down to rescue them.' 'I am sending *you*!' (Exodus 3.7–10).

Moses could not have been a more reluctant commissary. 'Lord, don't send me' (Exodus 4.10) he pleaded, and again,

'Lord, please send someone else' (Exodus 4.13). Yet he found himself both inspiring the Israelites and intimidating the Egyptians. He found himself leading an exodus from the land of slavery.

Those were awesome times. The power of the God of Israel seemed greatly in evidence. The Egyptians were beset by inexplicable disasters, some of them involving their own sacred symbols – the River Nile, frogs, beetles, cows, sheep, goats and even the sun itself. Death stalked the land. Amid the terror that all of this caused, the Israelites were allowed to leave and found themselves mysteriously able to cross the Gulf of Suez near a place called Baal Zephon on the western shore. When the Egyptians – who by then were having second thoughts – tried to pursue them, the attempt was a major catastrophe. The factors which allowed the Israelites to cross suddenly ceased to apply. Most of the Egyptian army was lost along with their heavy chariots and weapons of war. The Bible tells us that it was all connected with a strong east wind which 'blew all night and turned the sea into dry land' while it did so (Exodus 14.21). Meteorologists tell us that such a wind can still dry up the water, if combined with an ebbing tide, in this part of the Gulf. The timing was perfect for the Israelites. It proved deadly for the Egyptians.

God's promise to the Israelites, as entrusted to Moses and recorded in Exodus 6.6–7, was 'I am the LORD; I will rescue you and set you free from your slavery to the Egyptians. I will raise my mighty arm to bring terrible punishment upon them, and I will save you. I will make you my own people, and I will be your God. You will know that I am the LORD your God when I set you free from slavery in Egypt.' This promise was spectacularly honoured in the events which initiated the exodus. And initially, at any rate, the Israelites went on their way singing the praises of the great God who had delivered them.

I am reminded of a story about a little boy called David who attended a black Pentecostal church and who was totally captivated by the saga of the exodus. When it came up in the RE syllabus at the school he attended, he became a source of some irritation to his teacher because he kept on punctuating the lesson with shouts of 'Alleluiah!'

When his teacher asked him what all the noise was about, he replied, 'Alleluiah, miss. The Israelites done cross the Red Sea with the help of the Lord!'

Feeling that a little scholarly caution was appropriate, she corrected him, 'David, this was probably not the Red Sea but the Sea of Reeds, where the water was only four inches deep.'

David lapsed into silence, but not for long. Within minutes the alleluiahs were erupting again.

'Whatever is it now, David?' asked his teacher.

'Alleluiah, miss,' came the reply. 'The Lord done drown the whole Egyptian army in just four inches of water!'

The whole sequence of events is intriguingly mysterious and scholars continue to debate just what it was that took place in order to permit the Israelites to move out of their state of slavery and move on to the next stage in their history, but however it happened the Israelites were like David. They could recognize deliverance when they saw it.

> Then Moses and the Israelites sang this song to the LORD:
> 'I will sing to the LORD, because he has won a
>     glorious victory;
> he has thrown the horses and their riders into
>     the sea.
> The LORD is my strong defender; he is the one who
>     has saved me.
> He is my God, and I will praise him, my father's
>     God, and I will sing about his greatness.
> The LORD is a warrior; the LORD is his name.'
>                                           (Exodus 15.1–3)

This act of deliverance was crucially important for the foundation of the nation of Israel. The Israelites often looked back to it. They often saw echoes of it in their subsequent history. The principle became rooted in their national consciousness. Though life is a game of snakes and ladders, full of both ups and downs, throughout it all in one way or another *God delivers those who put their trust in him*.

However, speaking of snakes and ladders, there is a negative principle too, following logically from the positive one – the obverse side of the coinage of deliverance. As an illustration of it, how about the strange story of . . .

## Snakes in the desert

It is not only in Genesis 3 that a snake intrudes into Scripture. In fact snakes provide one of the recurring subthemes of the Bible. Perhaps this is not surprising. Humankind has always had trouble with snakes. Worldwide there are about 30,000 deaths a year from snakebites. Since the dawn of history snakes have been regarded with a mixture of fear, revulsion and awe.

The book of Numbers records a weird incident in which snakes play a central part. As the story starts in chapter 21, the Israelites are well into their years of nomadic life in the desert. Their memories of God's great act of deliverance from slavery in Egypt are beginning to fade a little. Their mental attitude is worsening. Gratitude is giving way to anger and resentment. They are full of complaints. We are told that 'the people lost their patience and spoke against God and Moses'. They grumbled, 'Why did you bring us out of Egypt to die in this desert, where there is no food or water?' (Numbers 21.4–5.)

This sort of miserable and negative spirit did nothing for their health and wholeness. When they were attacked by poisonous snakes, their natural immunity was low and 'many Israelites were bitten and died' (Numbers 21.6).

However, as often happens, the advent of a specific threat concentrated their minds and spirits and drove them back to faith. 'The people came to Moses and said, "We sinned when we spoke against the LORD and against you. Now pray to the LORD to take these snakes away"' (Numbers 21.7).

So Moses prayed for the Israelites and received a most unexpected piece of guidance. He was led to make a bronze snake and put it on a pole. Israelites bitten by snakes were to look at the bronze snake as an act of obedience to God and a means of finding healing. Scripture tells us that this is exactly what happened. 'Anyone who had been bitten would look at the bronze snake and be healed' (Numbers 21.9).

What are we to make of this odd story? Is it just a piece of ancient and unreliable folklore? Before we write it off as having no more than antiquarian interest, there are several points we should ponder.

According to St John, Jesus took this story very seriously indeed. He actually saw the snake on the pole as a symbol of his own ministry, a symbol of himself. 'As Moses lifted up the bronze snake on a pole in the desert, in the same way the Son of Man must be lifted up, so that everyone who believes in him may have eternal life' (John 3.14).

The promise of Scripture is that new life will surge within those who look upon Jesus in faith. The biblical expectation is that this new life will be demonstrated physically as well as spiritually. We are even told that if believers pick up snakes they will not be harmed (Mark 16.18)! St Paul demonstrated immunity to a snakebite before he conducted his Christian healing mission in Malta (Acts 28.3–9).

There are some Christian groups where these texts are regarded as having literal and present significance. When my wife and I visited North Carolina recently, we learned that there are flourishing sects in existence there, in which handling poisonous snakes is a regular part of worship. As I write I am looking at a selection of photographs taken at snake-handling services. The snakes are genuinely venomous and highly dangerous. Any attempt to make them less so is regarded as an affront to the Lord. We were told that a pastor who induced lethargy in his snakes by keeping them in an icebox was unceremoniously sacked by his congregation.

Is this faith or foolhardiness? Discipleship or derangement? Perhaps it is a sign of my cowardice, but I have to say that I feel no urge at all to prove my love of the Lord by handling poisonous snakes, and I would guess that your own feelings may be much the same as mine in this. If so, what lessons and conclusions can we draw personally from the Old Testament story of the snakes in the desert and the connected New Testament texts?

After many years of studying and seeking to practise the Christian healing ministry I have come to believe strongly that Scripture, experience and logic alike indicate that Jesus does have a healing impact on those who look to him in faith. My reasons are contained in *The Practice of Christian Healing* (Lawrence, 1998). If they are valid, all I would add here is that it should not be surprising if one of the effects of this healing impact consists of an enhancement of the immune system.

Perhaps we can also see some point in the nature of the symbol of healing that Moses created – the bronze snake on a pole. It is one of the mysteries of Christian healing that the causes of our hurts can paradoxically become channels of healing if they are offered back to God in faith and obedience.

As far as the negative principle is concerned, which is illustrated by the story of the snakes in the desert, it is certainly not difficult to see its relevance in a society like ours that harms itself so markedly by rejecting biblical standards.

It is a lesson not only of the experience of the Israelites but of human history as a whole that *we cannot turn our backs on God with impunity*. It brings disaster now, just as it did then.

Finally in considering this story it is important not to be so preoccupied with its negative aspects as to miss its healing content. Hard upon its negative message, it goes on to re-emphasize the positive principle with which this chapter started. No matter how great the mess we may create and the trouble we may invite by disobedience to God, it is never too late to repent, never too late to rediscover God's transforming and healing power.

## But can we really believe these stories?

Maybe before ending this chapter we ought to pause and ask an awkward question. You may well be feeling that this is the right time for a credibility test. Clearly the evidence of history suggests that the Israelites' escape from slavery was a truly remarkable event and it was to be expected that they would encounter venomous snakes in the desert. But what about the claim that some of those who were bitten were given an *instant* enhancement of their immunity system and that St Paul reproduced the same phenomenon years later? How credible is that?

Suppose we leave aside the testimony of Scripture for a moment. What about our own experience? Is there any evidence of comparable healing here and now?

I believe there is. Even in my own life and experience, with all its limitations, I know of occasions when the Christian healing ministry has had a similar impact. Of course, we do not come across many cases of snakebites in England, but there are often cases where the immune system needs to be reinforced. I have not only seen it happen, but I have seen it happen instantly.

For instance, in *The Practice of Christian Healing* I told the story of a dentist who, when in hospital with a life-threatening condition of double-virus pneumonia, found that his raging temperature immediately reverted to normal when I visited him and laid hands on him in the name of our Lord. The nurse who was responsible for taking his temperature every hour at first assumed that her thermometer must be broken and was quite shocked when she found that it wasn't.

Or consider this more recent incident. Not long ago I was invited to write two articles for a magazine on the subject of Christian healing. I used these articles to suggest a method by which readers might practise the presence of our Healing Lord in the expectancy that Christ has not changed and that his presence still brings new levels of life to us in body, mind and spirit.

Two or three weeks later a letter arrived in the post. It was from a physiotherapist. Let's call him 'Robert'. Robert had come across one of my articles while in hospital awaiting emergency surgery for a large pelvic abscess which almost completely surrounded his rectum. The evening before his operation, having read the article, he turned on a tape of some Christian music and found himself, in his own words, 'overwhelmingly aware of the presence and even the very touch of Jesus'. Next morning the surgeon found that the abscess had mysteriously disappeared. As a physiotherapist, Robert was able to obtain copies of the hospital documents dealing with his case. As I write, I have them on my desk in front of me. They give details of the rather gruesome condition with which he was admitted. They also include the operative record in the surgeon's own hand confirming that by the time Robert arrived at the operating theatre there was, 'no erethema, no swelling, no rectal horseshoe abscess, no pelvic abscess'. Robert comments, 'I was and still am amazed and filled with wonder. I have no pain despite the extensive investigation and I feel great.'

I found myself sharing his amazement – and yet perhaps I should not have been surprised. For it brought back memories of a healing I had received myself many years before. At the time I was plagued with boils. Horrible it was, and nothing seemed to make much difference. My GP prescribed antibiotics but they had little effect. Even with their help my immune system was totally unable to cope. So an appointment was made for me to see a skin consultant.

It was then that one of my colleagues, a priest from Nigeria with a firm belief in the healing ministry, turned up on our doorstep. He invoked the presence of Jesus and in a voice resonant with authority spoke directly to my crop of boils: 'In the name of God, *go – go – go!*' My immune system perked up instantly. The boils rapidly started to fade. I never did get to see the consultant!

So the apparently unlikely Old Testament story of snakes in the desert cannot be written off on the grounds of incompatibility with our own experience, and even though I am not in any way drawn towards joining the American snake-handlers, I cannot fail to note that journalists who investigate them often end up totally convinced that, though these sects are odd, on the whole they are *not* fraudulent. See for instance the report in *The Times* on Saturday 3 January 1998. It seems that believers bitten by poisonous snakes really do display again and again signs of an extraordinary enhancement of their immune system.

There is a mystery of sickness and there is a mystery of healing, whether we think in physical, mental or spiritual terms. If we would seek to probe that mystery, we cannot afford to ignore God's gift of experience – both the experience he gave to his chosen people, as recorded in the Bible, and our own experience too.

So before you turn to the next chapter, may I suggest that you pause and ask yourself, 'What does my own experience teach me? What are the things which I know from experience enhance me as a human being and make me more whole physically, mentally and spiritually? And what, by contrast, are the sort of things which I know from experience diminish and debilitate me as a human being and make me less than I might be?'

And then ask yourself just one more question, 'Why, in the name of God, can it be that so often I opt for the latter rather than the former?'

# CHAPTER FIVE

## *Laws of Healing*

Read Exodus 20.1–17
    Deuteronomy 30.15–30

Moses not only played a major part in the exodus and in many of the other experiences in the early history of the Israelites, but he was also crucially involved in the Jewish compendium of Law, contained in the first five books of the Bible. The Hebrew word for this compendium of Law is the *Torah*. According to my view of Scripture, it is the second of God's gifts to his chosen people. The Torah is made up of hundreds of individual precepts, remarkably comprehensive in their coverage of life. Some are sublimely spiritual and point to the heart of the Jewish faith, as for instance in the case of Deuteronomy 6.5 ('Love the LORD your God with all your heart, with all your soul, and with all your strength'). Others go to the heart of human relationships, as in Leviticus 19.18 ('Love your neighbour as you love yourself'). Others make no attempt to be sublime, but deal with a wide range of life's gritty practicalities (like Deuteronomy 23.12–13, which specifies the basic requirements for an outdoor loo, if you are camping!).

Back in Genesis 3, the talking snake convinced Adam and Eve that the way to have a good time was to break God's laws. It was a lie – but we still fall for it. We still confuse liberty with libertarianism. The motto for many is still 'to hell with the rule book' – even though if we reject God's rule book, then hell is precisely where we shall go, and there is quite enough hell on earth here and now to prove it.

The purpose of God's Torah is our wholeness. Its laws are laws of healing. This was made very plain to the Israelites at an early stage during their years in the desert. 'The LORD gave them laws to live by and ... said ... "I am the LORD, *the one who heals you*"' (Exodus 15.25–26).

Listen to the psalmist rhapsodizing about the Torah:

The law of the LORD is perfect; it gives new strength.
The commands of the LORD are trustworthy, giving
    wisdom to those who lack it.
The laws of the LORD are right, and those who obey
    them are happy.
The commands of the LORD are just and give
    understanding to the mind.
The worship for the LORD is good; it will continue for ever.
The judgements of the LORD are just; they are always fair.
They are more desirable than the finest gold; they are
    sweeter than the purest honey.
They give knowledge to me, your servant; I am rewarded
    for obeying them.

(Psalm 19.7–11)

The psalmist is right. The snake was wrong. History proves it. We could all see it easily for ourselves if the snake venom in our veins did not distort our spiritual vision. But as it is, we need a little help. So it is good to have the Torah. It offered healing insight to the Israelites of old. It can still offer guidance to us today.

## The Ten Commandments

The Ten Commandments, which were entrusted to Moses as

he meditated on Mount Sinai more than 3,000 years ago, provide a cross section of some of the Torah's central precepts. They can be found in Exodus 20.1–17 and again in Deuteronomy 5.1–22. These commandments used to be displayed in large print on the walls of most churches. But now most churches have painted them out. It is a mistake, I reckon – a serious one.

During World War II, signposts were removed throughout the United Kingdom. We knew that hostile invaders might come at any time and wanted to make life difficult for them. Removing signposts is a way of confusing your enemy, not a way of helping your friends. The Ten Commandments are important spiritual signposts and can guide us through life as long as they are in view. The devil can hardly have believed his luck when the churches started to paint them out!

Here now is a tiny contribution towards painting them back in again. You will notice that the first four commandments deal with our duty to God and the next six deal with our duty to each other. The translation, as in most of this book, is from the Good News Bible, though some readers may prefer to read them again in one of the older versions or in a traditional prayerbook.

## 1

'I am the LORD your God. Worship no god but me.' In other words – let God be God in both personal and national life.

## 2

'Do not make for yourselves images of anything in heaven or on earth or in the water under the earth. Do not bow down to any idol or worship it, because I am the LORD your God, and I tolerate no rivals.' There is no substitute for God. Nothing in this universe, wonderful though it is, can take God's place. You and I may not have totem poles in our back gardens, but there is no shortage of idols in the world today. Money, power, prosperity, popularity and glamour are all well-worshipped idols. We are stupid enough to treat these things and much more beside as though they were God. The result is disastrous.

Also with the true God out of the way, superstition can have a heyday. Some time ago I was involved in making a programme with a TV crew. During a coffee break some of the members of the production team started to tell me about their attitudes to life. None of them had time for traditional religion, which they regarded as totally out of date, but when I asked them whether they believed in anything at all one after another said that they believed (can you credit it?) in magpies! They said that if you see one magpie, it brings bad luck, but if you see two, you will have good luck. At first I assumed that this was a wind-up, that they could not possibly be serious – but they were. It seems we have a god-shaped hole in our soul, and if we take the real God out of it, before long we end up stuffing it with magpies – or worse.

### 3

'Do not use my name for evil purposes, for I, the LORD your God, will punish anyone who misuses my name.' This may seem a small thing, but care in using the name of God is not unimportant. For the mind can follow the mouth.

### 4

'Observe the Sabbath and keep it holy.' For the Jews the holy day was Saturday. The choice of day was linked to the creation story in Genesis. 'In six days I, the LORD, made the earth, the sky, the sea, and everything in them, but on the seventh day I rested. That is why I, the LORD, blessed the Sabbath and made it holy.' For Christians it seemed inevitable that the holy day must move to Sunday because Jesus rose from the dead on the first Easter Sunday, and this act of re-creation was even more wonderful in their eyes than God's original act of creation. But in both cases, the conviction was strong that keeping the Lord's Day special must be a matter of major concern. This is why many who take the Christian faith seriously are also decidedly unhappy about legislation which threatens the special nature of Sunday. They see an attack on the Lord's Day as an attack on the Lord.

### 5

'Respect your father and your mother.' In this instance the commandment has a promise attached to it: 'so that you may live a long time in the land that I am giving you'. The Bible has no time for ageist attitudes or practices. It teaches that we all have our places in society – the old, the young, as well as the various levels in between. If all are bound together within the solidarity of mutual respect, society will be solid too.

### 6

'Do not commit murder' – either actively as in the case of terrorist bombers, or passively as by letting people die in the Third World, simply because we do not care enough about their condition or are too mean to do anything about it.

### 7

'Do not commit adultery.' Adultery carries the death penalty in the Old Testament, and though we may recoil from that penalty as primitive and barbaric, it does no harm to remember that there is still a sense in which it does so in society today, because promiscuous sexual practices result in disease and death on a wide and horrifying scale in our own world.

When St Paul says 'Avoid sexual looseness like the plague!' (1 Corinthians 6.18, J. B. Phillips), he is not speaking just in metaphorical terms. Unless we give serious reconsideration to the traditional Christian sexual code at this point in our history, we put ourselves and our society at risk in a way that can hardly be overstated. The facts are plain, and yet there is a curious conspiracy of silence about them. One of our doctor friends believes that this conspiracy of silence is *the* single greatest threat at present to the life and health of our nation.

### 8

'Do not steal.' You and I may never have been up before a court on a charge of burglary, yet it is salutary to stop and consider how widely this commandment applies. It includes petty theft ('no one will notice'). It includes conventional theft ('everybody does it'). It includes the theft of time, as in the case of the employee who puts in fewer hours than he or she is paid for. It includes the theft of health, as in the case of the employer who disregards health and safety regulations. It includes the theft of credit, accepting praise for someone else's efforts. It includes making inaccurate tax returns. It even includes meanness towards God, withholding time, talents, and money, which have come from him and of which we are required by Scripture to return a portion to him. For that too is a sort of theft, if we take the Bible seriously (see Malachi 3.8–9).

### 9

'Do not accuse anyone falsely.' Don't tell lies, especially lies which hurt another human being. And don't give a ready ear to malicious gossip. Adolf Hitler said that the 'inspired lie' was an important part of his political strategy, but in the end many of these lies were exposed and played their own part in his downfall.

## 10

'Do not desire another man's house; do not desire his wife, his slaves, his cattle, his donkeys, or anything else that he owns.' The average Englishman can probably put a hand on his heart and swear that he has never coveted a donkey in his life. But what about another man's house? Or another man's wife? Or someone else's job? Or someone else's salary? Or someone else's success in life? And if we fall for the sin of covetousness, we shall find that a poison is released into our souls. We cannot be happy while we covet. On the other hand if we can manage to take pleasure in the good fortune of others we will not only be happier for it but healthier too.

## A matter of life and death

Once upon a time children were taught to recite the Ten Commandments. Learning them was regarded as a matter of mental and spiritual hygiene. I remember that when I was at my junior school, each member of the class was allocated one of the commandments to learn and required to recite it the next day. Mine was number five and it is still etched into my mind in its traditional form. 'Honour thy father and thy mother; that thy days may be long in the land that the Lord thy God giveth thee.'

It is very different nowadays. Not many of us know the general content of the commandments, let alone their exact wording. Some have never heard of them – like the jazz guitarist who, when asked by his vicar whether he knew the Ten Commandments, said, 'You whistle it, I'll play it!'

This is sadder than we may realize. All of the Ten Commandments are health rules. If we break them either deliberately or out of ignorance, we invite sickness at many levels of our being. We have seen, for instance, that breaking the seventh commandment can damage us physically, and that breaking the tenth commandment can damage us mentally and spiritually; that breaking the fifth commandment undermines family life, and that breaking the sixth commandment threatens the whole family of humankind. It is at our peril that we break God's laws and the appalling truth is that at present in British society we not only break every one of the Ten Commandments, but we actually *justify* doing so.

Recently a number of politicians representing differing persuasions have spoken of the urgency of recovering basic moral values – though some have backed off again, after coming to the conclusion that this might be electorally unpopular. They need our prayers both for perceptiveness and for courage. The Bible tells us that rediscovering God's laws is not only a matter of urgency, it is actually *a matter of life and death*.

Deuteronomy offers us this message from God. 'I am giving you a choice between good and evil, between life and death. If you obey the commands of the LORD your God, which I give you today, if you love him, obey him, and keep all his laws, then you will prosper and become a nation of many people . . . But if you disobey and refuse to listen, and are led away to worship other gods, you will be destroyed – I warn you here and now' (Deuteronomy 30.15–18). 'I am now giving you the choice between life and death, between God's blessing and God's curse, and I call heaven and earth to witness the choice you make. Choose life' (Deuteronomy 30.19).

Tough stuff! And if it is nonsense, we should of course

brush it aside and continue upon our permissive way. But if you have the feeling that, though it is unpalatable, it may not only be true but also crucially important, then here is a personal exercise to undertake before you leave this chapter. Read and ponder all Ten Commandments in your prayers day by day for a full week until God shows you some change, some development, some input which your own life requires. Then take action. I promise you it will be a healing exercise. It is true that there can be pain as well as joy in prayer and action of this sort. But the joy outweighs and outlasts the pain. For contrary to the devil's disinformation service, the psalmist does not deceive us when he says that in the long run God's law is 'sweeter than the purest honey'.

# CHAPTER SIX

## *Healing Worship*

### Read Psalm 103

It was good for the people of Israel to have the benefit of centuries of experience to enable them to discern their way forward. It was also good that many of the lessons which experience taught them were encapsulated in the Law that Moses brought them. But they needed more than this if they were truly to be the people of God. They needed an interior strength, which could only come from an actual encounter with the God who had called them. So his third gift to them was the opportunity to meet with him in the mysterious activity which we call worship.

During the years that followed the exodus, they developed a pattern of worship that was suited to their nomadic lifestyle. It was centred upon a special tent, known as the 'Tabernacle' or 'Tent of Meeting'. We are told that God said to Moses, 'The people must make a sacred tent for me, so that I may live among them' (Exodus 25.8). Nothing but the best of materials were used for its furnishings and contents. At its heart was a wooden box, covered in gold, containing the stone tablets on which the Ten Commandments were etched (Exodus 25.16). There was also a golden lampstand (Exodus 25.31–40) and an altar where sacrifices could be offered to God (Exodus 38.1–7).

However, though the furnishings were as ornate and

precious as circumstances permitted, in the last resort a tent is still a tent. So when the Israelites became a settled people, occupying a territorial kingdom, their third king, Solomon, son of David, built a temple in Jerusalem (1 Kings 6) and, as the centuries went by, this was supported by a network of local synagogues.

We are very fortunate that five major worship books used in the temple have been preserved for us. These books have been put together in what we know as the Psalter or the book of Psalms. The Israelites found the Psalter full of inspiration and of healing.

The psalms, many of which go back to King David and beyond, have two main characteristics. They make it their aim to be totally true to God, but they also seek to be totally true to life and experience and, because there is a continuity in life and experience across the centuries, they are as relevant to us as they were to the Israelites. Whatever our mood of the moment, the odds are that we can match it within the Psalter and take it and ourselves into God's presence to seek his restorative power.

One of the marks of the Psalter is that it acknowledges the fact that, though Scripture teaches that God delivers those who trust him and that those who disobey him do so at their peril, these truths are often far from apparent in the world as we know it. A fallen world like ours can be a cruel place. Bad things can happen to good people.

In such a world, what sort of worship could be relevant and therapeutic? First, say the psalmists, worship should be totally honest. Worship means bringing our real selves to God, no matter how negative our feelings may be about life and indeed about God.

This is a conviction which is totally consistent with Scripture as a whole. Listen to Moses, for instance, as he speaks his mind to God in no uncertain way. 'LORD, why have you treated me so badly? . . . Why have you given me the responsibility for all these people? I didn't create them . . . I can't be responsible . . . it's too much . . . If you are going to treat me like this . . . kill me, so that I won't have to endure your cruelty any longer' (Numbers 11.11–15).

Or how about Jeremiah? Just listen to him, as he hides absolutely nothing of his disappointment and doubt, when he approaches God in prayer. 'Why are you like a stranger in our land, like a traveller who stays for only one night?' (Jeremiah 14.8.) 'Why do I keep on suffering? Why are my wounds incurable? . . . Do you intend to disappoint me like a stream that goes dry in the summer?' (Jeremiah 15.18). 'LORD, you have deceived me' (Jeremiah 20.7). 'Cursed be the day I was born!' (Jeremiah 20.14).

In the same way, the psalmists take their fears, their failures, their frustrations straight to God. Again and again the psalms reflect the dark side of life – anguish (22), shame (51), fear (55), anger (88), personal disaster (13), national crisis (89), and much more besides. It is not surprising that Gideon Bibles, which contain a well-known list of Scripture texts to read in times of trouble, rely heavily on the psalms. The Gideon list contains more texts from the psalms than from all four Gospels put together.

However there is a second and more fundamental conviction in the Psalter. Having come to God, just as we are, and ventilated our pain and outrage in his presence, we shall find that God will lead us through them into a new awareness of his healing nature and often, rather to our surprise, into a spirit of praise. Real pain and real praise – we find them both in the Psalter.

Some psalms go straight into a praise mode and, because it is deeply therapeutic to affirm the highest and the best, it seems right that now, if we would find healing in the Bible, we should look at a psalm of praise in some detail.

## Psalm 103

Psalm 103 is a meditation upon and a response to the Bible's teaching about God's love.

### Verse 1

Praise the LORD, my soul!
All my being, praise his holy name.

In the Bible the word 'name' does not just indicate a tag by which someone is known. In Hebrew thought one's name is somehow part of one's nature. So when the psalmist asks that he may praise the name of God with all his being, he is defining his aim in worship precisely and ambitiously. What he longs to do is to savour God's essence and in doing so to apply the *whole* of his own being to acknowledging and enjoying all that God reveals to him. He is aiming at the ultimate in positive perception and positive response. He asks that his own heart may be one with the heart of reality. In a sense this is a risky prayer. For he knows that at the heart of reality there is awesome holiness. But he is prepared to take the risk, because he is also convinced that at the heart of God, along with this holiness, there is also an amazing kindness:

### Verse 2

Praise the LORD, my soul,
and do not forget how kind he is.

When I first entered the ministry dozens of people wrote to me offering a wide range of advice for the future. The letter I remember best came from a refugee from Hungary. On 23 October 1956 there had been a courageous uprising in Hungary against Soviet domination. University students had demonstrated, demanding democracy. Huge crowds joined them. The secret police fired on them, but the whole nation seemed to join the uprising and the Soviet troops withdrew. For one heady week the democratic parties were reconstituted. Cardinal Mindszenty was released from prison. The whole nation basked in a new sense of hope and freedom. But on 30 October 1956 the Soviet mechanized troops rolled back in. The country was immersed in a bloodbath. Soviet domination was re-established. However, 160,000 refugees escaped and one of them wrote to me. I shall never forget his words. 'Teach your people to be kind,' he wrote. 'Kindness is what this world needs.' I have expanded his words into a full chapter in my book *Make Me a Channel* (Lawrence, 1996), but here I would just make the point that kindness is an underrated quality. It is sometimes confused with weak sentimentality, but nothing could be further from its true nature. The psalmist reminds us that kindness is part of the essence of Godhead. In the words of W. H. Faber, 'The heart of the Eternal is most wonderfully kind.'

The psalmist then goes on to remind us that to encounter the God whose essence is both holiness and kindness is a profoundly healing experience.

## Verse 3

He forgives all my sins
and heals all my diseases.

We are damaged people living in a damaged world, but at the heart of the Christian faith there is the good news that God's will is for our healing, both spiritually and physically. It is in fact logical that worship should be a healing experience. If God exists and creativity is of the essence of his being, and if he is totally self-consistent (as is emphasized, for instance, in James 1.16–18), then when he encounters that which is damaged his creativity must show itself as re-creativity or healing, and to contact him in worship must increase our level of wholeness.

This ought not to be possible because our impurity and his holiness are incompatible, but he enables the impossible to happen by the miracle of forgiveness. We shall not understand how this miracle can happen until we move on to the New Testament with its mysterious teaching about the power and purpose of the cross of Christ, but the psalmist foresees that there must be a desire for forgiveness and reconciliation at the heart of a God of love, and this conviction brings him a sense of liberation and of rejuvenation:

### Verses 4–5

He keeps me from the grave
and blesses me with love and mercy.
He fills my life with good things
so that I stay young and strong like an eagle.

In France not so long ago Europe's oldest woman celebrated her 120th birthday. One of my doctor friends tells me that this sort of lifespan could be much more common, were it not for the fact that we shorten our years on earth by lifestyles that ignore not only the laws of God but also the principles of common sense. It would seem that the psalmist's words about the power of worship to lengthen life can be taken quite literally. It even seems that medical research may be beginning to prove this statistically.

However, I have to say that because I take the biblical promise of eternal life seriously, I have no great longing to achieve extreme old age. For me Psalm 103 speaks of something more important. One of the remarkable things about Christian faith and life in our experience is that as you get older on the outside, you actually become younger on the inside.

My wife, Eira, and I are both in our sixties, and on the day on which I am writing these words we are celebrating 40 years of marriage. Eira has found an anonymous quotation for me to include in the speech which I shall soon be making at our Ruby Wedding party. It is worth reproducing here. Its subject is:

### Youth

Youth is not a time of life. It is a state of mind.
It is not a matter of ripe cheeks, red lips, supple knees.
It is a temper of the mind, a quality of the imagination,
    a vigour of the emotions.
It is a freshness of the deep springs of life.
Youth means a temperamental predominance of
    courage over timidity,
of the appetite for adventure over love of ease.
This often exists in a man of fifty more than in a boy of
    twenty.
Nobody grows old by living a number of years, only by
    deserting their ideals.
Years wrinkle the skin, but to give up enthusiasm
    wrinkles the soul.
Worry, doubt, self-destruction, fear and despair are the
    long, long years,
that bow the head and turn the growing spirit to dust.
Whether seventy or sixteen there is in every being's
    mind
the love of wonder, the sweet amazement at the stars,
the starlike things and thoughts, the undaunted
    challenge of events,
the unfailing childlike appetite for 'what next?' and the
    joy of the game of life.

You are as young as your faith, as old as your doubts,
as young as your self-confidence, as old as your despair.
In the centre place of your mind there is a radio station.
So long as it receives messages of beauty, hope, cheer,
    courage,
grandeur and power both from earth and from the
    infinite infinite –
So long are you young.

This is the sort of youthfulness that really counts. For Jesus says that achieving youthfulness of spirit is an essential part of our preparation to be citizens of the kingdom of God (Mark 10.15).

So in the verses we have considered so far there is good news for sinners, for the sick and for the aging. There is also good news in this psalm for the oppressed:

### Verses 6–7

The LORD judges in favour of the oppressed
and gives them their rights.
He revealed his plans to Moses
and let the people of Israel see his mighty deeds.

It is sometimes said that there are two types of Christians, those who are keen on worship and on all that goes on in church and those who are much more concerned about matters of social justice and human rights. This should be a false distinction, because the God to whom we draw close in worship is the God who in the words of Bishop David Sheppard has a 'bias towards the poor'. Christian worship should be a spur to our social conscience. Or to put it the other way round, our social conscience should be stimulated and sharpened by the contact which we have with our just and holy God in worship.

If any branch of the Christian Church fails to share God's bias to the poor, it not only betrays the poor but betrays Jesus himself. This is powerfully stated in James 2.1–9. Any church which gives the best seat to the 'rich man wearing a gold ring and fine clothes' breaks God's Law and displays motives that are actually evil, says St James. There is similar teaching at the heart of the Magnificat, Mary's song of praise in Luke 1.46–55. The God of both the Old and the New Testaments is a God who has 'scattered the proud', 'brought down mighty kings', and 'lifted up the lowly'. He proved it, says Psalm 103, by his dealings with Moses and the enslaved Israelites. It is small wonder that when there was slavery in the American deep south, so many of the spirituals which the slaves loved to sing took their theme from the exodus. 'Let my people go' (Exodus 8.1) is still God's command to all who victimize and brutalize their fellow humans.

The God of Scripture would be well pleased with organizations such as Anti Slavery International (Thomas Clarkson House, The Stable Yard, Broomgrove Road, London SW9 9TL; Tel: 020 7501 8920; Website: http://www.antislavery.org/); or Christian Solidarity Worldwide (PO Box 99, New Malden, Surrey KT3 3YF; Tel: 020 8942 8810; Website: http://www.csw.org.uk) for which the president, Baroness Caroline Cox, so often provides what her biographer, Andrew Boyd, calls 'a voice for the voiceless'; or Relief for Oppressed People Everywhere (12 Church Street, Rickmansworth, Herts WD3 1FP; Tel: 01923 771821; Website: http://www.rope.org.uk) and with many others too. But would he be pleased with you and me?

It is so easy to be lukewarm in our concern for suffering humanity, particularly if the suffering is taking place some distance away from us. Bertram comes to mind, in many ways a lovely and gentle Christian man but with a total blank spot as far as the world beyond his own neighbour-hood is concerned. He gives generously to his parish church, but he stipulates that none of his gifts should go to missionary societies or other non-local causes. If we are like that, not only do we defraud our fellow human beings but we diminish and damage ourselves too. That is the clear message of Jesus in Matthew 25.31–46. Why not pause for a moment and read his words?

And there's more, much more in Psalm 103 – but we must deal with it more briefly. The rest of the psalm tells how God can be moved to anger by human sin, but fortu-nately for us his love is greater than his anger (verses 8–11). God, we are told, is in the removal business. It is his will to remove our sins from us as far as the east is from the west (verses 15–18). He has the power to do so, because he is King of all creation, King of both time and eternity. However before we receive the full benefits of his kingship personally, we must enthrone him in our own lives (verses 19–22). And so the psalm ends as it begins: 'Praise the LORD, *my* soul!'

If we spurn the gift of worship, we may well find our-selves living our lives inside a hall of mirrors, and distorting mirrors at that. It is a small room, dank and unhealthy. However, if we hear and heed the Bible's call to worship, we can break out into a wider world, a world where the air is fresh and healthy, where the horizons are infinite and where, as Psalm 103 reminds us, our voices mysteriously blend with those of angels, archangels and all the host of heaven.

The healing potential of worship comes from the com-pany that we keep as we pray and praise God's holy name – and I do not just mean our fellow worshippers in the church down the road. The human tragedy, as we saw in our earlier studies in Genesis, is a tragedy of separation. We were meant to be one with God and his universe and all that is in it, but because of our sin and disobedience we have become separated from him, from each other, from the created universe and from all that is in it, including the depths of our own inner selves. We have become poor lonely souls, wilting away within our self-imposed isolation. The triumphant conclusion of Psalm 103 celebrates the reunion which awaits me when I lift my soul in praise to the Lord. For all who serve him on earth are doing the same. So are all who serve him in realms beyond this earth. The more deeply I worship, the more completely I become one with the essence of life. And as I join the host of those who rejoice to enter the presence of the King of creation, what else should I expect but that the scars of my separation should begin to heal in my body, in my mind, in the life that I live, in the person that I am, and ultimately within the spiritual entity that I am called to become in the shining mystery of eternity?

## CHAPTER SEVEN

# Wisdom, Prophecy and a Special Promise

Read Proverbs 3.7-8; 4.20-22
     Job 42
     Amos 1 and 2
     Hosea 1—3
     Isaiah 11.1-9; 52.13—53.12

Historical experience, a special code of Law and the inspiration which can come from worship – these were the initial gifts of God to the Israelites. But there was more to come. Before the end of the Old Testament era they were to receive three further gifts, all of which were rich in their potential for healing. There was the practical guidance of those who wrote what became known as the wisdom literature. There was the powerful and challenging ministry of the prophets. There was also a very special promise.

## A word from the wise

Rightly or wrongly the Jewish king, Solomon, had a great reputation for wisdom, and much of the wisdom literature is associated with his name, just as many of the psalms bear the name of King David. The best-known examples of this literature comprise Proverbs, Job and Ecclesiastes in the Bible and Ecclesiasticus and the Wisdom of Solomon in the Apocrypha.

There are perhaps two major points that the wisdom books are concerned to make, and we need to absorb both if we are to take advantage of their healing potential. One is that *God gave us common sense so that we might use it and benefit from it*. One of the effects of turning away from God is a weakening of common sense, a loss of the capacity for straight thought and clear vision, an inability to live according to the principles of practical wisdom. The wisdom literature seeks to reaffirm those principles. It aims to help us to make life work out in practice.

It teaches that to accept a biblical philosophy of life brings healing. The book of Proverbs guarantees that this is so. It says, 'Never let yourself think that you are wiser than you are; simply obey the LORD and refuse to do wrong. If you do so, it will be like good medicine, healing your wounds and easing your pains' (Proverbs 3.7–8). Or in the more memorable if somewhat quaint translation of the King James Version, 'Be not wise in thine own eyes; fear the LORD and depart from evil. It shall be health to thy navel, and marrow to thy bones'! Or how about Proverbs 4.20–22? 'Pay attention to what I say, my son. Listen to my words. Never let them get away from you. Remember them and keep them in your heart. They will give life and health to anyone who understands them.' The King James Version says, 'My son, attend to my words; incline thine ear unto my sayings. Let them not depart from thine eyes; keep them in the midst of thine heart. For they are life unto those that find them, and health to all their flesh.'

The commonplace accusation that some religious people are 'so heavenly minded as to be of no earthly use' could never be levelled against the book of Proverbs. Its aim is to reveal and re-establish God's own common sense in the nitty-gritty details of everyday life. Again and again it shows that it knows about those details with a degree of uncomfortable perceptiveness. For instance, its description of the hangover that can follow a binge has never been bettered. You can read it in Proverbs 23.29–35.

However, the writers of the wisdom literature are far from simplistic. They know that life is complicated and often messy. They are just as honest as the writers of the psalms. Though they are totally convinced that accepting a biblical philosophy of life does you good at every level of your being, they know full well that it does not always seem so. At the heart of the wisdom literature there is the book of Job with its unparalleled exposé of the enigma and agony of innocent suffering.

Job is a pious family man and is wealthy and healthy till Satan strikes him down. Poor Job loses his health, his wealth and his family. His friends come round and advise him to try to understand, because if he can fathom why these things have happened, he will be able to amend his life and all will be well. Job knows that the situation is nothing like as simple as that. He and his friends argue themselves to a standstill, and it is at this point that God finally speaks. Strangely he says nothing about Job's sufferings but just takes him on a tour of creation and helps him to see the mystery of it all. Finally Job makes the discovery for himself that if there are mysteries in the whole creation process, there must be other mysteries too – including the mystery of suffering. He stops trying to understand. He settles for a sense of mystery. There are, he says, 'marvels too great for me to know' (Job 42.3).

At the end of the story he finds new wealth, new health and a new family. But first he has to learn that *there are times when our trust has to be greater than our understanding*. This I take to be the second major theme of the wisdom literature.

## God's publicists – the prophets

In spite of the agonies of the book of Job, much of the wisdom literature is communicated in a tone rather like that of a college seminar or a family fireside chat. However, there are times when, if God is to get through to us, he has to turn up the level of volume. This brings us to his fifth gift – a gift delivered with fire and passion by his servants and publicists, the prophets.

There were prophets amongst the Israelites back in the days of Moses and even earlier. But though in the case of many other Jewish leaders the earliest were regarded as the most important, so that for instance Abraham was thought to be the greatest patriarch and Moses the greatest law-giver, it was not so with the prophets. Samuel, who does not appear in the pages of history till the later part of the eleventh century BC when he was involved in the foundation of the monarchy, is usually regarded as the first of the great prophets. He was followed in the ninth century BC by Elijah and Elisha. They in turn were followed by further prophets of major significance in the eighth century onwards. We are fortunate that much of their teaching has been preserved in the books at the end of the Old Testament.

The essence of their work was to perceive and proclaim the significance of events in the world around them. They were given insight into the principles of cause and effect and so could often see how history was developing and what the future would bring. Because of this we tend to think of them as *foretellers*, but it is more accurate to regard them as *forthtellers*. When the united monarchies of Saul, David and Solomon split into a northern and a southern kingdom, both kingdoms had their prophets. Amos and Hosea warned the people of the north that they were guilty of widespread disregard of God's law and that, unless there was national repentance, disaster would follow. Events proved them to be right. The Jews of the north were conquered by the Syrians in 722 BC and were scattered throughout the world. Jeremiah and Isaiah warned that a similar fate could befall the southern kingdom. Once again the prophetic insight proved to be true. Jerusalem fell in 586 BC and most of the people had to endure 50 years of exile in Babylon. The prophetic ministry continued throughout and beyond these years of exile.

The prophets understood and expounded the two basic principles which we have already identified as fundamental to Jewish life and law – that God delivers those who put their trust in him whereas those who turn their back on him invite disaster. Affirming and interpreting these truths did not make them popular. Jeremiah in particular was hated and reviled. We still describe the bearer of a message we would rather not hear as a 'Jeremiah'. Yet the prophets deserved a better reception from their compatriots. For they were the bearers of healing to those who had eyes to see and ears to hear.

Some of the prophets had a personal healing ministry which foreshadowed that of Jesus. Elijah healed a widow's son by a mixture of prayer and what may have been a version of the kiss of life (1 Kings 17.8–24). It was a mysterious healing which was later to be reproduced by Elisha (2 Kings 4.8–37). Elisha also was the agent through whom healing came to Naaman, a Syrian general, who was a leper (2 Kings 5.1–19). Isaiah helped to save the life of boil-stricken King Hezekiah in a healing that involved both prayer and poulticing (Isaiah 38)!

For the most part, of course, the ministry of the prophets was one of proclamation, but again it was proclamation with a potential for healing, whether it seemed positive or negative in tone. This can be seen in the two examples that follow.

## Amos 1 and 2

If you had been around the sanctuary at Bethel between 760 and 750 BC, you might have seen a rather neat prophetic psychological coup. For Amos managed to make the Israelites open their ears to a distinctly unpalatable message. He stalked into the sanctuary in his shaggy shepherd's clothing, a gaunt contrast to the sleek businessmen who were regularly to be found there, and immediately collected a large crowd around him by prophesying a highly unpleasant end for Israel's less popular neighbours.

'The people of Damascus have sinned again and again', says the Lord, 'and for this I will certainly punish them.' Amos listed the sins of Damascus and specified the coming punishment – and then immediately changed his target.

'The people of Gaza . . . The people of Tyre . . . The people of Edom . . . all have sinned again and again and for this I will certainly punish them.' The crowd grew. National pride was in the air.

Again and again the formula was repeated. Nation after nation came under the denunciation of the prophet and the sentence of God. 'The people of Ammon . . . The people of Moab . . . they have sinned again and again and for this I will certainly punish them.' The crowd continued to swell. Then it caught its breath. Here was something better still.

'The people of Judah have sinned again and again and for that I will certainly punish them.'

The Israelites of the northern kingdom wasted no affection on the Judeans of the southern kingdom. They were often at war with them. So to hear a prophet classify Judah alongside Damascus and Ammon and Moab and the rest of the pagan world was an immensely gratifying experience. But then Amos dropped his bombshell.

'The people of *Israel* have sinned again and again and for

that I will certainly punish them.' In condemning Damascus, Ammon, Moab and Judah, the Israelites had condemned themselves. For they were guilty of equal offences and merited the same judgement.

The rest of the book of Amos largely consists of prophecies and visions of judgement. It was precisely, said Amos, because the Israelites had been so intimately known and cared for by God that their sins were so appalling (Amos 3.2), and inexorably he applied God's laws of cause and effect to those sins. As he did so, he found himself predicting a future of self-inflicted pain for the people to whom he prophesied.

Yet the book of Amos ends with words of hope (Amos 9.11–15), and I see no necessity to assume, as some Bible scholars do, that these have been added by a later hand. For in Amos, as in so many of the Old Testament messages of judgement, there is an underlying awareness of the love of God and a conviction that God never ceases to offer healing to those who turn to him.

This positive side of prophecy is shown very clearly by our next illustration, taken from the life and ministry of one of the most remarkable of the Old Testament prophets.

## Hosea 1—3

The first three chapters from Hosea tell the story of an extraordinary man who lived an extraordinary life. It would make a sensational film or TV series. The personal drama and the psychosexual dynamics are so intense that it is surprising it was not snapped up by the media years ago.

Hosea's wife Gomer was repeatedly unfaithful to him. Adultery became an addiction for her and she left her husband for a life of prostitution, which ultimately led her into destitution and slavery. Hosea was revolted by all she was doing, and yet he found he could not stop loving her. So his book tells how he bought her back for himself and offered her another chance.

As he wrestled with his own love and his own anguish, the conviction came to him that there was a parallel between Gomer's behaviour towards him and that of the Israelites as a whole towards God. God had pledged himself to the people of Israel but in return Israel had often been unfaithful, broken his laws, embraced false gods, bowed down before idols, and gone the way of disgrace and self-destruction. Hosea, like the other prophets, had often denounced this treacherous pattern of behaviour. And yet, as he thought about his own wife, it came to him strongly that God could not love Israel less than he himself loved Gomer. If he longed to rescue Gomer, God could not have less of a longing to rescue Israel.

Of course God would regard the sins of Israel with abhorrence, and as his prophet Hosea denounced those sins with passion. And yet though he pictures Israel languishing in what he calls 'Trouble Valley' (Hosea 2.15), he cannot help but imagine God opening up 'a door of hope' right at the heart of that valley. For all Israel's disobedience and betrayal, it is God's healing will to win her back. If only Israel will respond once again to the God who delivered her from slavery in Egypt and whose will is to deliver her again, then God will restore her. 'Israel,' he will say, 'I will make you my wife; I will be true and faithful; I will show you constant love and mercy and make you mine for ever. I will keep my promise and make you mine, and you will acknowledge me as LORD' (Hosea 2.19–20).

So here is a paradox. The God whose holiness must ultimately destroy all evil nonetheless offers hope and healing and new life to all who will hear him and receive his gifts. Hosea speaks of both God's wrath and God's love. But on the basis of his own experience, he knows with certainty that the love is greater than the wrath. Read Hosea 11.1–9. Or compare Hosea 13.7–9 with 14.4–8. Hosea's God is above all a God of healing.

## Four healing truths

It is time to pause again in our scriptural survey and consider how the wisdom literature and the prophets speak personally to us in our search for healing in the Bible. Out of the many truths they offer us, here are four.

1   When the wisdom literature seeks to increase our openness to ordinary common sense, this is a matter of some importance and even of some urgency to society today. The paradoxical thing about 'common' sense is that it isn't! Common sense is actually rather rare. Again and again it is disregarded by large sections of society. For instance, it is not sensible to invite addiction by experimenting with drugs. Neither is it sensible to risk serious disease because of sexual promiscuity. Then again, it makes no sense to pollute our planet and universe in the way that we do. It makes no sense to invite lung cancer by smoking. It makes no sense to damage ourselves by overeating and overdrinking. It makes no sense to cherish resentment and hatred when these things poison the mind, harm the body and endanger society. It makes no sense to embrace a materialism which puts things before people. The wisdom writers are speaking to our own nation, and to you and me personally within it, when they say, 'In God's name, *stop* and *think*!' The prophets with their insight into cause and effect say much the same thing. We need urgently to rediscover the truths which they saw so clearly. We need to pray for a new

breed of prophets to help us do so both nationally and individually.

2  We would do well to learn from the way in which the Old Testament prophets were often rejected. If someone offers us a potentially healing insight into ourselves, it is important to be aware that we may not instantly welcome it. We often prefer the comforting lies of a flatterer to the painful truths of a friend. It is worth while pausing here and now to ask, 'Am I at this moment in life resisting a painful truth which a good friend has offered me?'

3  It could be that your personal need at this moment is to look again at the book of Job. You may be trying seriously to follow the precepts of common sense. You may also be striving to lead a godly life. You may be open to hear truth, even truth that is hard to bear. And yet in spite of all these things, life may be difficult and painful. This may be because of illness. It could be because of adverse circumstances. Speaking personally, I have suffered from a bad back for two years. During this time I have been told of several people who have been healed of back problems at services which I have conducted – but my own problem is still with me. So what am I to say to myself? And what am I to say to the many people who live in circumstances much worse than mine and have conditions to bear that are much more serious than a backache? What if they have prayed earnestly for healing, and no healing has yet come?

I must not offer any glib or superficial answer. The friends of Job meant well, but they had little to teach him. He was in fact nearer to God than they were, though he did not feel it, and he was right in his conclusion that in this mysterious world there are many circumstances and experiences which are totally beyond our comprehension. As it happened, there was light at the end of the tunnel, but it was in the darkness that he grew in spiritual stature.

It was in one of Job's bleakest moments, after he had listed his troubles and pains and raged against God's apparent cruelty towards him, that he found himself saying, 'But I know that there is someone in heaven who will come at last to my defence. Even after my skin is eaten by disease, while still in this body I will see God. I will see him with my own eyes, and he will not be a stranger' (Job 19.25–27).

In other words, in the midst of his pain he acknowledged the mystery of life, he acknowledged the God whose ways he could not understand, and he went on living life a day at a time. This is not the message we like to hear when we are in trouble. But sometimes, for reasons which we cannot fathom, it is – for a time at any rate – the only message that is available.

4 However, what the Bible does tell us is that in the times of greatest darkness, whether that darkness is self-induced or not, we can still – as Hosea taught – discover and be discovered by God's love. And if we invite that love into the centre of our lives, the Bible guarantees that his love will make a difference. Even if initially nothing changes externally, the healing power of God will be in evidence internally, at the very heart of our trouble. The acknowledgement of God's loving and healing presence will institute a new and transforming cause-and-effect sequence. Who knows what then may follow?

Patrick, a Roman Catholic priest, told me that he is actually thankful for the cancer that threatened his life. For without it he does not believe he would have come to his present knowledge and experience of God. In his case he went on to make a complete recovery. But I also think of Greta who discovered God's love as she was dying from her cancer. The discovery did not prevent her death, but it was a joy and a privilege to watch the stirring of a new dimension of life in her during her final days and to be with her and her family as she prepared to enter eternity with a total freedom from the fear and rage which had filled her beforehand.

However, I wonder if at this moment you feel you want to say something like this to God: 'All this talk about your love sounds very good. But talk is cheap. Think of Hosea! He did not just talk about love. He actually showed it and he paid the price for doing so. What we actually need is for you to come and show us this much-vaunted love of yours in action.' If so, then read on.

## A special promise

We have almost come to the end of our tour of the Old Testament. There are many omissions in it. There have been no references, for example, to the lessons that can be learned from the adventure stories contained in books like Joshua and Judges early in Israelite history and the book of Esther at a much later stage. We have neglected the love story told by the book of Ruth and the love poetry in the Song of Solomon. We have paid scant attention to the history of the Jews while they were ruled by kings, or to their years of exile in Babylon, or to their eventual return to Jerusalem, to the rebuilding of the city walls and the temple and the rest of the post-exilic history. This story can be read in the two books of Samuel, the two books of Kings, the two books of Chronicles and then in Ezra and Nehemiah. But there can be no time or space for it here.

However, before leaving the Old Testament, we must

consider God's sixth gift to his chosen people. In addition to their historic experience, their sacred law, their way of worship, their wisdom literature, and the ministry of the prophets, they received a further and final gift of a very special promise.

The conviction grew among them that there would come into their midst a child who, as his life developed, would be uniquely commissioned and empowered for God's purpose to save and heal this damaged world. They had a name for this coming one. They called him the 'Messiah' or 'Christ', which means 'the anointed one'. Others with a more limited commission for God had already received an anointing to authorize their work. So Saul and David were both anointed by Samuel for their role as kings (1 Samuel 10.1 and 16.13). But the one who was to come as God's final gift to his chosen people would not just be *an* anointed one. He would be *the* anointed one. In a way that was completely unique he would be the righter of wrongs, the healer of hurts, the bearer of new life, the Saviour of the world.

Scriptural references to him are mysterious and enigmatic. Some stress the wonder of such a person as king and judge, the reconciler of all that has been created, the bringer of peace and joy. Read, for instance, Isaiah 11.1–9. Other references contain a strange and foreboding sense that the messianic mission cannot be fulfilled without fearsome pain. So Isaiah 52.13—53.12, which is traditionally regarded as a description of the Messiah, speaks of him as a suffering servant – horrendously afflicted, despised and rejected, yet from whose wounds will flow a life stream which can bring about the healing of self-tormented humankind. In both joy and pain, we are told that healing will be the Messiah's purpose. God gives this promise through the prophet Malachi: 'For you who obey me, my saving power will rise on you like the sun and bring healing like the sun's rays.'

Or in the lovely traditional words of the King James Version, 'Unto you that fear my name shall the Sun of Righteousness arise with healing in his wings' (Malachi 4.2).

As we move into the New Testament we shall see Jesus of Nazareth claiming this messianic role for himself. He quoted the words of Isaiah 61: 'The Spirit of the Lord is upon me, because he has chosen me to bring good news to the poor. He has sent me to proclaim liberty to the captives and recovery of sight to the blind; to set free the oppressed and announce that the time has come when the Lord will save his people' – and to the fury of many of his hearers he applied this text to himself (Luke 4.18–21). John the Baptist, whose prophetic ministry bound together the Old and New Testaments, endorsed this claim and gradually disciples gathered round Jesus, united in the conviction that 'We have found the Messiah' (John 1.35–40).

Jesus was prepared to die rather than abandon his messianic claim (Mark 14.61–64), and as now we turn to his story, it is for each one of us to make up our own mind about its validity, knowing as we do so that, if millions of Christians throughout the centuries are to be believed, whether or not we manage to find healing in the Bible depends in the last resort on whether or not we manage to discover *him*.

# CHAPTER EIGHT

# *The Healing Christ*

Read John 1.1–14
      John 4.1—5.19

We come now to the high point in our search for healing in the Bible – and indeed, if the Christian faith is to be believed, to the high point in human history. We come to Jesus of Nazareth, the healing Christ.

In my earlier books I have usually drawn most of my material from the first three Gospels, when considering the healing ministry of Jesus. Matthew, Mark and Luke tell stories of healing with such simplicity and vividness. Anyone wishing to have a crash course on the healing ministry of Jesus could do no better than read the first ten chapters of St Mark's Gospel. They tell a dozen individual stories of healing and contain several references to multiple healings as well. In the words of Mark 6.56, 'Everywhere Jesus went, to villages, towns, or farms, people would take those who were ill to the market places and beg him to let them at least touch the edge of his cloak, and all who touched it were made well.' The first three Gospels show Jesus as one who was consistently infectious with wholeness.

However, in the interest of balance, in this chapter my intention is to concentrate on St John's Gospel. In many ways it reminds me of the creation stories of Genesis, which we considered earlier in this book. The early chapters of

Genesis begin by viewing creation on a cosmic level and then narrow their focus to tell us how Adam, God's prototype man, lost his wholeness. Similarly, St John's Gospel tells a re-creation story, which begins at a cosmic level and then focuses on the life and ministry of Jesus, who came to be the prototype of a new humankind, and who offers the prospect of wholeness restored to all who will receive it.

## Jesus – the Word of life

'In the beginning God created the heaven and the earth . . . and God said, "Let there be light."' So it is that Genesis begins in the traditional translation of the Bible, and John deliberately echoes these words in the way in which he opens his Gospel. 'In the beginning was the Word, and the Word was with God, and the Word was God . . . In him was life; and the life was the light of men' (John 1.1–4, AV). The word that God spoke in the Genesis creation story is personalized in John's story of re-creation. Jesus *is* that creative and re-creative Word. 'The Word was made flesh, and dwelt among us (and we beheld his glory, the glory as of the only begotten of the Father), full of grace and truth' (John 1.14, AV).

In Genesis, after the camera has panned the cosmic scene, it then zooms in for a close-up and we find ourselves standing beside the stream which waters the Garden of Eden (Genesis 2.10). In John's Gospel after the cosmic opening we find ourselves standing beside the River Jordan, watching Jesus being baptized by John. The cosmic dimension has not quite gone away. John the Baptist testifies that Jesus existed long before he himself was born, because Jesus is God's own Son (John 1.30, 34). Back in Genesis 1, we are told that at the moment of creation the Spirit of God moved on the face of the water as God's creative agent (Genesis 1.2). John's

Gospel tells us that the Holy Spirit came upon Jesus as he was baptized and remained with him as a re-creative agent for his mission as Messiah (John 1.32).

Soon we are told that the re-creative work of Jesus is to offer an opportunity for damaged human beings to be born all over again. So low have we fallen that nothing less will suffice. This was the message of Jesus to the Jewish leader, Nicodemus, when he came to pay a furtive nocturnal visit. 'No one,' said Jesus, 'can see the Kingdom of God unless he is born again' (John 3.3).

The Nicodemus story is also notable for containing some of the most famous and best-loved words in the whole of the Bible. 'God so loved the world, that he gave his only begotten Son, that whosoever believeth in him should not perish, but have everlasting life. For God sent not his Son into the world to condemn the world; but that the world through him might be saved' (John 3.16–17, AV). We could just as easily translate the end of that quotation as 'but that the world through him might be healed'. For the Greek word *sozo* means 'heal' as well as 'save'. The re-creative process for which Jesus came into the world is comprehensive in its application. It does not just apply to our inner self and to our eternal prospects. It is concerned with all we are and all we do and all we may become. It certainly has wonderful implications for our eternal destiny, but while it is preparing us for that destiny, it also affects our bodies, minds, spirits, relationships, attitudes and lifestyles here on earth.

So it is that St John's Gospel – just like the Gospels of Matthew, Mark and Luke – is concerned to illustrate the healing difference, in all its fullness, which Jesus makes to all who are open to his presence and influence, and we can see this if we look in rather more detail at some of the stories which he tells in chapter 4 and in the earlier part of chapter 5.

## Jesus makes a healing difference

### John 4.1–4

As we join John's narrative, he draws a word-picture for us of Jesus on the move. Actually, though we rarely hear it mentioned, it does seem that Jesus had a little house at Capernaum. In his home town of Nazareth many felt resentful about the young man who claimed to be Messiah. 'We know him and his family,' they said, and rather ruefully Jesus commented, 'A prophet is never welcomed in his home town' (Luke 4.24). Some felt so badly about him that there was an attempt on his life (Luke 4.28–30), and since 'not even his brothers believed in him' (John 7.5), 'he did not stay in Nazareth but went to live in Capernaum, a town by Lake Galilee' (Matthew 4.13). It looks as if the house that had its roof demolished, when a paralysed man was lowered into his presence by four friends, belonged to Jesus himself. For in the words of the Good News Bible, Jesus 'was at home' at the time (Mark 2.1). But during the three years of ministry at the end of his life, it seems he was not at home very often, and at the beginning of John 4, we find him forgoing home comforts and travelling the 70 miles from Judea to Galilee along the dusty road on foot.

### John 4.5–6

We catch up with him in Samaria at a town called Sychar and perhaps the first thing that strikes us about him is that Jesus is completely exhausted. It is a noticeable feature of John's presentation of the gospel that, though it seems that out of all the four evangelists he is the one who is most concerned to present the cosmic and eternal glory of Jesus as Co-creator of the universe, simultaneously he stresses how vulnerable Jesus was during his earthly ministry. Though he is Messiah, he is a Messiah who can be hungry, thirsty and tired, a Messiah who has no immunity to physical, mental or spiritual suffering.

## John 4.7–8

In his weariness Jesus has flopped down at the side of a well. The disciples have gone off to buy food. Jesus would have loved some water from the well, but a bucket was needed before water could be drawn. It was at this point that a Samaritan woman arrived, carrying a bucket. John tells us that Jesus asked her for a drink, but then events developed in a most unexpected way. Though Jesus was physically parched with thirst, he soon discerned that here was a woman who was *spiritually* parched, and so it happened that, thirsty as he was, Jesus found himself offering the woman the spiritual refreshment of the water of life. We are told that this was a woman with a bad reputation. Pious Jews would have shunned her. But though we sometimes refuse to be on speaking terms with Jesus, he never refuses to be on speaking terms with us. We snub him (God forgive us), but he never snubs us. So Jesus and the Samaritan woman talked together and, thanks to St John's Gospel, we can eavesdrop.

## John 4.9–16

Jesus – Would you mind if I had some water from your bucket?

Woman – You're a Jew, aren't you? Don't you know I'm a Samaritan? Are you sure you want to use *my* bucket?

(She knew that normally Jews and Samaritans had nothing to do with each other. A Jew would never drink from a Samaritan's cup or eat from a Samaritan's bowl. Jews had an apartheid policy towards Samaritans, whom they regarded as half-breeds and heretics. But it is at this point that the conversation took an unexpected turn . . .)

Jesus – If only you knew who was asking you for water, you'd be asking me!

Woman – You can't get water. You've not got a bucket.

Jesus – I'm not talking about water from this well. I'm talking about water that will last for ever, the water of eternal life.

Woman – I could do with that. I'm fed up with bringing my bucket to the well.

Jesus – Go and get your husband and I'll explain it to both of you . . .

## John 4.17–26

(We can imagine an awkward pause here. The Samaritan woman could see that the conversation was moving onto dangerous ground and so she answers Jesus with a half-truth.)

Woman – I haven't got a husband.

Jesus – I know. You've had five, haven't you, and the man you're living with now isn't any of them.

(The going was getting hot for the woman at the well, so at this point she tried to move the conversation onto safer ground. She poses what from her point of view was a nice non-threatening religious question . . .)

Woman – I see you're a prophet. So answer me this. We Samaritans have always worshipped God on our local mountain, but the Jews say God can only be properly worshipped in Jerusalem. What do you think?

(We love questions about the externals of worship. We will talk endlessly about whether worship should be formal or informal, about organs versus guitars, about what the inside of a church should look like, about what vicars should wear, and the like. Religious externals seem safe and non-threatening things compared to personal questions like the direction of our own lives and the state of our own souls.

But Jesus will not allow this or any other conversation with him to become bogged down in externals.)

Jesus – The only worship that counts is living worship, true worship.

(The woman prepares to beat a retreat, but offers a religious platitude before she goes . . .)

Woman – Oh, well, I expect that when the Messiah comes, he'll explain everything.

(Then comes the bombshell . . .)

Jesus – I *am* the *Messiah*.

## John 4.27–42

Just then the disciples returned. They were surprised to find Jesus talking to the Samaritan woman. They were even more surprised when she completely forgot about her bucket and ran back into the town to tell others about the man she had met. But the biggest surprise of all was when the townsfolk flocked out to listen to Jesus. He had clearly made a difference to the woman at the well. The implication of the text is that she became a believer and we are told that many of the townsfolk became believers too. The story ends with their words to the woman, who found she had started what then expanded into a two-day mission to the people of Sychar. 'We believe now, not because of what you said, but because we ourselves have heard him, and we know that he really is the Saviour of the world' (John 4.42).

## John 4.43–54

St John has already referred in general terms to miracles performed by Jesus (John 2.23), but it is not until he has dealt with the spiritual needs of Nicodemus in chapter 3 and the emotional needs of the woman at the well in chapter 4 that John allows himself to tell a story of physical healing. However, he does so now. After his mission in Sychar, Jesus moved on to Galilee, where he was approached with a request for the ministry of healing by a government official, whose son was at the brink of death. John does not tell us of any physical contact between Jesus and the sick boy. What John does report is that a word of power spoken by Jesus was sufficient to activate all the healing that the boy needed.

## John 5.1–9a

John follows this story immediately by reporting an incident set in Jerusalem at the side of a pool which was thought to have healing properties. The theory was that if the water was stirred by the wind, the first person to bathe in it after-wards would find healing. There, beside the pool, was a man who had been ill for 38 years. He never managed to be the first one into the pool. Whenever the water stirred, somebody who was more nimble got in ahead of him. Jesus saw his long-term plight, talked with him about his need for healing and then, completely ignoring the pool, spoke another word of power. 'Get up,' he said, 'pick up your mat, and walk,' and we are told that immediately the man became well and was able to walk away.

## John 5.9–19

Subsequently Jesus sought out the man and impressed upon him that healing of the body does not in itself bring whole-ness. There must be healing of the mind and soul too. As for the Jewish authorities, John tells us that they could see no further than the fact that the healing work of Jesus and the subsequent carrying of a mat by the healed man constituted a technical infringement of the Sabbath, when no work of any sort was permitted. Jesus pointed out that God the Father was always at work, even on the Sabbath, and that the same must apply to him too. This made them angrier than ever. They felt that 'not only had he broken the Sabbath law, but he had said that God was his own Father and in this way had made himself equal with God' (John 5.18). The chapter ends with Jesus patiently explaining his life-giving messianic role to them, but realizing as he does so that their ears and hearts are closed to him.

We can almost feel St John grieving for them. For in spite of the stories of healing contained in chapters 4 and 5 of his Gospel and even more remarkable healing stories in chapters 9 and 11, John is less concerned to catalogue such events than to reveal the essential nature of the Messiah. So, under John's guidance, it seems right now to reflect on some of the basic truths he reveals about Jesus. For it is only as we begin to understand the nature of the Christ, that we can also begin to understand the nature of Christian healing.

## What sort of Messiah was Jesus? – Seven answers from St John

### A divine and mysterious Messiah

Jesus, says St John, is a Messiah clothed in mystery – glorious, cosmic, eternal, divine. We sometimes have a tendency to scale down the essential wonder of all that Jesus is and does, but on grounds of logic, as well as of faith, I am convinced that the Johannine perspective is absolutely right. It is not in any way confined to John's Gospel. The divinity of Jesus, with all its cosmic and eternal implications, is also a theme to be found consistently throughout the New Testament. Jesus is the 'visible likeness of the invisible God' (Colossians 1.15). 'He reflects the brightness of God's glory and is the exact likeness of God's own being' (Hebrews 1.3). Jesus is quite simply 'God with us' (Matthew 1.23). I have written more fully about this conviction in *Journey into Mystery* (Lawrence, 1999) and *Christ with Us* (Lawrence, 1997). All

I would add here is that the healing ministry of Jesus follows naturally from his oneness with the Father because, as we have already seen in our survey of the Old Testament, the will and work of God the Father is inextricably connected with the healing of his damaged creation.

## A vulnerable and human Messiah

Paradoxically John also stresses that Jesus is a vulnerable Messiah. Though Jesus is 'the Father's only Son' (John 1.14) and 'is the same as God' (John 1.18), yet there is nothing ersatz or phoney about his humanity. We have already noticed his tiredness, his hunger, his thirst at the well in Samaria. All the Gospels portray him as experiencing the limitations of human nature – temptation, disappointment, depression, physical weakness and pain, emotional distress, anguish of spirit, and even, as he hung on the cross, the feeling that he was God-forsaken. John makes it plain that Jesus ministers God's healing from the heart of his own vulnerability, and a similar vulnerability has been a fundamental element of genuine Christian healing throughout the centuries. As I write these words, my friend and colleague, Russ Parker, Director of the Acorn Christian Healing Trust, is recovering from a time of debilitating illness. This is how he reflects upon it in the final Acorn magazine of the old millennium: 'Jesus never used his intimacy with God to shield himself from the trials of being fully human. This serves to remind us that in the healing ministry we cannot hide from ourselves or pretend to be what we are not. When we are tempted to play the game of always being strong or never having a need in front of those we seek to serve, we should remember the example of the supreme wounded healer.' It is at the point of maximum vulnerability, as he hangs on the cross, that Jesus shows himself most powerfully as the healing Messiah, and it is not till he has accomplished his mission of suffering that he allows himself the triumphant cry, *Tetelestai* – 'It is complete!', 'Finished!', 'I've done it!' (see John 19.29).

## A surprising Messiah

If the combination of divinity and vulnerability is surprising in John's description of the Messiah, this is consistent with the whole of the story of Jesus, as John tells it. For the Messiah, as John perceived him, was full of surprises. John's Gospel moves from one surprise to another. The first miracle which John records, the changing of water into wine at a Galilean wedding feast (John 2.1–12), was certainly highly surprising. None of the other Gospel writers record it. Jesus' message to Nicodemus in John 3 was equally surprising. The final words of the dumbfounded Jewish leader are, 'How can this be?' We have seen how Jesus surprised the woman at the well in John 4, and John specifically records the surprise that the disciples felt at that encounter and its consequences. The Jewish authorities were surprised at Jesus' healing ministry (John 7.21), and Christian healing is a ministry which surprises us to this day. We should beware of those who seem to imply that its nature is predictable. I well remember an occasion when a woman in hospital who I was told by the ward sister was 'as good as dead' made an instant recovery after I laid hands on her in the name of Jesus, and yet at about the same time a common cold from which I was suffering proved completely resistant to the healing ministry!

## A Messiah committed to the healing of the human spirit

There are, however, general principles which John offers us about the Messianic healing ministry. We have seen that one of them is that spiritual wholeness is more important than physical wholeness. Jesus was concerned for both of them, but there is no doubt where he placed his prime emphasis. It is vital that this sense of perspective be maintained within the Church's healing ministry today. A hospital administrator once promised me that he could fill my church, if only I would moderate the gospel challenge which was always a key ingredient in our healing ministry. He was impressed with the healing impact which he had heard we could have on people who came to our services but felt that what he termed 'all the Jesus stuff' would put many off. I have to admit that just for a moment I looked over into the abyss of temptation, but not for long. The Jesus stuff is what Christian healing is about – and I told him so. It was good to hear subsequently that in time he came to see this for himself and that he is now a committed Christian.

## A Messiah concerned with the whole of life

Having said that the human spirit is the key concern of the ministry of Christian healing, it must be added that Jesus is a Messiah for whom there is no such thing as a no-go area. Everything that I am, everything that you are – physically, mentally, emotionally, spiritually – is his concern. He is concerned about us individually, he is concerned about us corporately. He is concerned about our homes, our neighbourhoods, our society, our nation, our world, our universe. Nothing is irrelevant to him, nothing is beyond his reach. His will is to make a healing difference to all that is damaged or hurt, and the healing ministry he offers is never lacking in point, purpose or power, no matter how hopeless or chronic a condition may be, and no matter how unsuitable anyone who comes for help may seem. The first physical healing recorded by John is that of an apparently hopeless case, for the official's son in John 4 was at the point of death. And conditions do not become much more chronic than that of the man involved in the second physical healing, for the man by the pool in John 5 had been ill for 38 years. All the Gospel writers make the same point. Nothing repels or intimidates Jesus, where there is pain and need. He touches lepers, ignoring the physical risk entailed. He does not shrink from contact with a corpse, ignoring the ritual defilement that this involved. It caused outrage when he invited a variety of 'sinners' into his presence. Many of them not only began to experience a completely new quality of life because of his influence, but became channels of that new life to others. Many of the early 'saints' were anything but saintly before they encountered Jesus. Matthew, who collected taxes for the hated Roman occupiers, would have been regarded as a quisling and a cheat. Simon Zelotes was a freedom fighter, a terrorist, sworn to kill people like Matthew. Mary Magdalene is traditionally thought to have been a prostitute and was certainly a woman of dubious reputation. But it was the way of Jesus to take on people and problems of every sort, and to leave a trail of healing behind him.

## A Messiah able to speak 'a word of power'

Jesus was able to do these things because there was power in his word. The concept of Christ's 'word of power' is central to St John's Gospel. At the beginning of time, primordial darkness could not resist him (John 1.4–5), and during his earthly ministry his word proved stronger than disease and death (John 4.45—5.18). Yet if human beings used their free will to close their ears to his word, he respected their right to do so, and for this reason he knew what it was to fail. He could do little for the authorities at Jerusalem or for many of the local people in his home town.

## A Messiah whose work continues

Finally John makes it abundantly clear that Jesus is a Messiah whose healing work will continue and even expand through his followers. Listen to these truly amazing words of his. 'Whoever believes in me will do what I do – yes, he will do *even greater things*, because I am going to the Father. And I will do whatever you ask for in my name, so that the Father's glory will be shown through the Son' (John 14.12–13). But can we conceivably bring ourselves to believe it? As our search for healing in the Bible continues, our next question has to be, 'Does Jesus *really* heal today? And if so, how?'

# CHAPTER NINE

# Does Jesus Heal Today?

Read Luke 8.1—9.6; 10.1–20
    Acts 3.1–16; 5.12–16
    James 3.14–16
    Matthew 18.20; 28.16–20

To the question 'Does Jesus heal today?' the New Testament answers with a resounding '*Yes*'. For its pages contain not only extensive evidence of Christ's own healing ministry but also details of the commission which he gave to his followers that they too should be the bearers of Christian healing.

St Luke, traditionally thought to have been a doctor, provides a mini-handbook of both the ministry and the commission in three consecutive chapters of his Gospel. Luke 8 tells the story of a mission of preaching and healing undertaken by Jesus himself. The preaching includes the parable of the sower, and three startling healings are recorded. A deranged man in a graveyard is restored to his right mind. A woman with a chronic haemorrhage is healed merely by touching Jesus' robe. A little girl in a deep death-like coma is restored to life. Then in Luke 9 this startling ministry is delegated to the 12 apostles. We are told that Jesus 'sent them out to preach the Kingdom of God and to heal the sick' (9.2) and, probably to their own amazement, 'the disciples left and travelled through all the villages, preaching the Good News and healing people everywhere'

(9.6). St Luke is at pains to point out that the apostles were far from super-saints at this stage. He pictures them as deficient in understanding (9.45), in humility (9.46) and in love (9.54) and yet the healing ministry is placed in their hands. When we move into Luke 10, not only does the delegation process continue but it expands. For we are told that Jesus sent out all the followers who happened to be with him at the time – 72 in number – on a similar mission. His words of commission were 'heal the sick' and 'say to the people . . . "The Kingdom of God has come near you"' (10.9). Once again the mission is crowned with success. The 72 come back rejoicing (10.17) and Jesus rejoices with them (10.21).

Ultimately all believers were to be called to share in this Christian healing ministry (Mark 16.18) and in the Acts of the Apostles we are given details of the response of the early Church to that call. Just as during the time of our Lord's earthly ministry, so during the apostolic age, 'Crowds of people came in from the towns around Jerusalem, bringing those who were ill or who had evil spirits in them; and they were all healed' (Acts 5.16).

## Acts 3.1–16

It may be helpful to look at an instance of apostolic healing in greater detail. The case of the lame man to whom Peter and John brought the healing power of Christ in Acts 3 is particularly interesting because it closely parallels one of the miracles of Jesus which we have already considered: the healing of the lame man by the pool, as told in John 5.1–19.

John's pool was located near what was known as the 'sheep gate' in Jerusalem. The healing in Acts 3 took place near another gate, the so-called 'beautiful gate' of the temple.

The man by the pool was a chronic case. He had been ill for 38 years. The condition of the man at the beautiful gate was even more chronic. He had been lame all his life.

Jesus healed the man at the pool with a word of power. 'Get up, pick up your mat, and walk' (John 5.8). A similar word of power is spoken by Peter in Jesus' name at the beautiful gate. 'In the name of Jesus Christ of Nazareth, I order you to get up and walk!' (Acts 3.6).

There was instant healing at the pool (John 5.9). There was instant healing at the beautiful gate also (Acts 3.7).

Jesus was careful to explain the power which had been at work in the healing at the pool. He was himself the source. 'What the Father does,' he said, 'the Son also does' (John 5.19). Peter too was careful to explain the nature of the power involved in the healing at the beautiful gate. He disclaimed any special personal prowess or holiness, as he said, 'Fellow-Israelites, why are you surprised at this, and why do you stare at us? Do you think it was by means of our own power or godliness that we made this man walk?' (Acts 3.12). He stressed that all the glory must go to Jesus. 'The God of Abraham, Isaac, and Jacob, the God of our ancestors, has given glory to his servant Jesus' (Acts 3.13). It is only by reference to Jesus that Christian healing can be understood. 'It was the power of his name that gave strength to this lame man. What you see and know was done by faith in his name; it was faith in Jesus that has made him well, as you can all see' (Acts 3.16).

These words of St Peter are of central importance in studying the Christian healing ministry. He identifies two resources, one greater and one lesser. The greater resource is what he calls 'the power of the name of Jesus', which in terms of the idiom of the Bible means *Jesus himself*. In Scripture a 'name' (*shem* in Hebrew, *onoma* in Greek) is no mere tag by which you are designated, but it somehow encapsulates your whole nature. 'The name of God' means 'God'. So when in the literal language of the King James Version Jesus says to God the Father, 'I have manifested thy name unto the men which thou gavest me' (John 17.6), the Good News Bible correctly translates this as 'I have made *you* known to those you gave me.' Knowing this idiom can make a significant difference to our understanding of Scripture. So, for example, the third commandment about taking God's name in vain means failing to reverence him and hallowing God's name in the Lord's prayer means standing in awe before God. Similarly when Peter tells us that Christian healing happens by the power of the name of Jesus, what he is saying is that the practice of the presence of Jesus himself lies at the heart of this ministry. The process of Christian healing is activated when real need is brought into real contact with the real nature of the living Christ.

The second and lesser resource is that of faith on our part. It is not that our faith 'does the healing', but it provides a link to the healing Christ in much the same way as an electric flex cannot in itself make any of our household gadgets work but it can provide a link to the power supply in the mains. Note that in the scriptural healing ministry the onus of faith is on the ministrant and not on the recipient. 'Those who believe shall lay hands on the sick' (see Mark 16.18); not 'Hands shall be laid on those who believe.' Of course if the recipient also has faith, that is a bonus, but it is not a requisite. Thus in Jesus' healing mission in Luke 8 the woman healed of her haemorrhage was able to exercise faith, but the little girl in the deathlike coma was neither able nor required to do so.

Once the resources of Christian healing are clear in our minds, it also becomes clear that those resources are not locked up in the pages of Scripture. They are available today. The fact of the presence of Jesus among his followers is guaranteed by his own promise, 'Where two or three come together in my name, I am there with them' (Matthew 18.20). All that remains for us to do is to accept his word and by that act of faith to connect the hurting world with the healing Christ.

But it is time for another credibility test. How can we know that this promise can be trusted and that Jesus truly can be with us today? If we are to have faith in it, what is the foundation for that faith?

## Christ with us

The concept of the presence of Jesus among his followers is a fundamental element of Christianity. It is not an optional extra. I have written about it in some detail in my earlier book, *Christ with Us* (Lawrence, 1997).

It rests upon four basic gospel truths. First, there is the Christmas truth that God has come among us. Jesus Christ was born into this world to lead a solidly historical life. Then there is the Good Friday truth that in spite of the sin and the horror which characterize human nature and human history, he did not turn away from us. His mission was to offer us a healing relationship and to pay the price of doing so. Next there is the Easter truth. We could not have a relationship with a corpse, but after Jesus had been brutally put to death, he was mysteriously raised again. Death could not hold him. You cannot keep a God-man down. Finally there is the truth we are called to celebrate at Ascensiontide. During his earthly ministry Jesus was only in one place at a time. Even during the 40 days after the resurrection the same seems to have been true. But at the ascension all spatio-temporal restrictions were removed, and the final words of Jesus according to St Matthew contained the solemn pledge on which the ministry of Christian healing and much more rests: 'I will be with you always, to the end of the age' (Matthew 28.20).

It is these four truths, presented to us at Christmas, Good Friday, Easter and Ascensiontide, which constitute the distinctive nature of the Christian faith and it is these four truths which provide the theological basis of the miracle of Christ with us today. There is no greater challenge for the Church as it moves into the third millennium than to rediscover and reclaim this gospel miracle and to explore all that follows from it. The Christian healing ministry is just one of its consequences. If it is true that Jesus went about 'preaching the Good News about the Kingdom, and healing people who had all kinds of disease and sickness' (Matthew 4.23), and if he has not changed but is 'the same yesterday, today and for ever' (Hebrews 13.8), then his presence *must* be a healing presence. We should not be surprised if healing takes place when we encounter him in Christian life and worship. Logically we should be surprised if it does not!

As we rediscover the Christ who is with us, it is also important to be aware that to encounter Jesus involves an encounter with God the Father and God the Holy Spirit too. 'The Father and I are one', said Jesus (John 10.30). 'Whoever has seen me has seen the Father... I am in the Father and the Father is in me' (John 14.9–10). And, as the Nicene Creed reminds us, the Holy Spirit proceeds from the Father and the Son. We have the guarantee of Jesus that the Father will 'give the Holy Spirit to those who ask him' (Luke 11.13). The Holy Spirit 'will be in you' (John 14.17, NIV). Once again the healing implications are plain. Our Father-Creator is also our Re-creator, 'the Lord ... who heals' (Exodus 15.26), and the Holy Spirit (to use the words of the Creed again) is 'the Lord and Giver of Life', the one whose work and nature it is to increase the level of life in every part of our being (Romans 8.6).

## Meeting Jesus

But what of the test of experience? Does it actually happen, this process of meeting with Jesus, which brings with it access to the healing power of the Holy Trinity?

It may come as a surprise to learn that many people have claimed this experience over the years. In New Testament times there was Paul's famous encounter with Jesus on the road to Damascus. The details are recorded in Acts 9.1–9 and again in Acts 22.6–10 and 26.12–18. But we do not have to delve into the distant past for experiences of this sort. Many people can be found who will testify that they can still happen – and can sometimes do so in a way that is audible, visible and tangible.

The Reverend George Bennett, who was a mentor to me and to many others in the rediscovery of Christian healing today, had a remarkable experience early in his ministry. He was driving his car in the outskirts of Coventry and while crossing the bridge over the Avon he felt a hand on his shoulder and heard a clearly audible voice, giving him a specific instruction which was to alter the course of his life. When he turned round, there was nobody there, but he was always convinced that this was a direct message from the Lord. The story is told in his book *Miracle at Crowhurst* (Bennett, 1970).

An even more remarkable story is told by Fred Lemon, who became a notable evangelist and communicator for Christ. In his earlier life he was a confirmed and violent criminal, but on the eve of an intended attempt to break out of Dartmoor he had an extraordinary experience. The story is told in some detail in his book *Breakout* (Lemon, 1977). 'Suddenly there were three men in the cell with me; they were dressed in ordinary civvy suits. The man on the right spoke – "Fred," he said, "this is Jesus." The middle figure at whom he pointed began to talk to me. Gently, clearly, he traced my whole life up to this desperate day.' The final words from Jesus were, 'If you want to become a Christian, you must drive out the hatred from your heart.' Then the three men faded and were gone. The experience changed Fred Lemon's life.

Something similar happened back in the seventeenth century to Samuel Rutherford, who was put into prison for his beliefs as a Presbyterian. In a letter to his parishioners he wrote, 'Jesus Christ came into my prison cell last night and every stone in it glowed like a ruby.'

Such occurrences are still reported, and occasionally I am privileged to hear of them. A few months ago a friend phoned me to tell me of an experience which she had during a time when she was having to cope with feelings of depression. She was on her way to her local station to take a train to her work in the heart of London, when suddenly she realized she was not alone. Jesus himself was walking at her side. He accompanied her to the station and sat with her on the train. She was able to talk with him about her life and not surprisingly this was a healing experience. In her own words, 'It was so natural and yet so extraordinary. The overwhelming thing was knowing he loved me exactly as I was.'

We never know when the Lord will cause his presence to be discerned. Just over a year ago a poorly little girl experienced healing at a service which I helped to lead in a Cheshire parish church. Subsequently when I mentioned this to someone who had been in the congregation at the time, her reply was, 'Well, it isn't surprising. You did see Jesus, didn't you? He was waiting for you as you came down the pulpit steps and walked with you to the sanctuary where you laid on hands.'

I have to say that personally I had not seen anything unusual at all. I would dearly love to experience the presence of the Lord visibly, audibly, tangibly. But so far I have never done so. Nonetheless I firmly believe in Christ with us. That is why I had no hesitation when invited to write a book with that title, and it is why for many years I have felt able, and indeed compelled, to conduct Christian healing services at which very many people tell me they have been healed or helped. I have just received a note bringing greetings from a professional violinist who a few years ago attended some healing services at St Stephen's, Prenton, where I was vicar. Some time beforehand she had fallen downstairs and damaged her neck, spine and shoulders. The condition deteriorated till she could hardly move her left arm. Orthopaedic specialists failed to help her and there was doubt whether she would play again. But after receiving the ministry of healing she found her range of movement was restored and she was able to resume her professional career. I still hear from her from time to time. Here, as always, healing had nothing to do with any healing gifts on my part. It had everything to do with the promised presence of Jesus.

## Practical hints about healing prayer

So if at this moment you and I need the healing touch, the healing love, the healing presence of Jesus, what can we do about it?

First, we must not despise the ministry of the church down the road from us. We can know that he is to be found there within the worship, because he says so (Matthew 18.20). The practice of Christian healing has been at the heart of the life and worship of the Church since its birth. The letter of James provides insight into the sort of healing ministry which characterized early Christian congregations.

Is any one of you sick? He should call for the elders of the church to pray over him and anoint him with oil in the name of the Lord. And the prayer offered in faith will make the sick person well; the Lord will raise him up. If he has sinned, he will be forgiven. Therefore confess your sins to each other and pray for each other so that you may be healed. (James 5.14–16, NIV)

Once again it is worth emphasizing that 'in the name of the Lord' means 'by contact with the Lord's own nature, by practising the Lord's living presence'. Anointing is a symbol of union with the Christ, the Messiah, the Anointed One. When hands are laid on, the body of Christ is giving the touch of Christ. When there is deliverance, it is his presence which drives out evil. Forgiveness comes by the power of his sacrifice on the cross. Healing prayer is no more and no less than bringing ourselves and all for whom we have a concern into his presence, so that he may infect us with his own unique wholeness. If the church down the road holds what are termed 'healing services', all these truths should be embodied within them. But in any case all Christian worship must have healing potential if, as the Bible teaches, its essence is an encounter with Jesus himself. If we would be biblical Christians, we must upgrade the level of our expectation of our churchgoing. Meeting Jesus always makes a healing difference to those who are prepared for it and for him. We should expect nothing less.

Then when we leave church, we certainly should not leave behind an awareness of his presence. He will 'walk with us and talk with us', if we invite him to be our companion along life's way. We will experience his friendship within our personal prayer life, and though it is good for there to be set times at which we concentrate on prayer day by day, there will also be a real sense in which those prayers will never cease because the friendship out of which they arise never ceases itself. Also because friendship is meant to expand and develop, our personal prayer life should never be static. It should be a journey of exploration.

I have already written fairly extensively about the experience of healing prayer in *How to Pray when Life Hurts*, in *The Practice of Christian Healing* and in *Journey into Mystery* (Lawrence, 1993; 1998; 1999), but because I believe that we are called continually to learn and move and grow in our prayer life, may I share with you a newly discovered prayer method. It came to me as I was reading about the famous French psychologist Émile Coué, who used to teach his patients to say 15 or 20 times a day the words, 'Every day in every way I am getting better.' (*Tous les jours, a tous points de vue, je vais de mieux en mieux.*) In the past this has always struck me as a rather pathetic exercise, no more than wishful thinking, which in spite of the re-creative power of the human mind may or may not in fact prove true. However, in the closing weeks of the old millennium, the conviction came to me that for Christians there is a spiritual exercise which, though it has something in common with the Coué practice, is better and stronger and more realistic. It emerges from the heart of our faith and we should be able to undertake it with total conviction.

I invite you to try it for yourself. During the weeks and months ahead, every day, slowly and deliberately say the words, 'Every day in every way Jesus is my Healer.' Or if you would like an occasional variation, try, 'Every day in every way the Father re-creates me.' Or 'Every day in every way the Holy Spirit heals me.' Then, if you feel moved to do so, as a consequence, you could add Coué's own words as a post-script. All of this should be done within an awareness of the promised presence of Christ and of the healing purpose of the Holy Trinity, and having undertaken this exercise at the heart of our prayers we can then offer it on behalf of others too.

Already I have some evidence of the healing power of this prayer exercise, but it is so simple that the easiest way for you to assess it is for you to try it for yourself. In preparation for it you may like to read again the story of Robert in Chapter 4, 'The Gift of Experience'. The essence of the healing ministry lies, to use Robert's own words, in becoming 'overwhelmingly aware of the presence and even the very touch of Jesus'. Please God, this awareness may invade the whole of the Church afresh, as we enter the new millennium. For the world needs the promised presence of Christ, perhaps as never before. And, please God, you and I may be part of this awareness, as we develop our own relationship with Jesus.

# CHAPTER TEN

# Questions and Answers

Read 2 Corinthians 12.1–10
    Ephesians 6.10–17
    Philippians 3.10–14
    Revelation 22.1–2

After the Gospels and the Acts of the Apostles, the New Testament continues with a sequence of letters, many of them by St Paul, and then comes to its conclusion with the strange and sensational book of the Revelation of St John the Divine. The purpose of these letters and to some extent of the book of Revelation was to answer the questions and meet the needs of the newly created Christian churches. Many of these questions and needs were connected with the ministry of healing.

All who are involved in Christian healing today know, if we are honest, that it is a ministry bristling with problems and difficulties. You may well have questions of your own and will do no service to the Lord of truth if those questions are suppressed. Personally I am very grateful that many of the issues about which I have a concern today were also a concern for the writers of Scripture, especially those to whom we owe the second half of the New Testament. Here then are some of my own questions, connected with the healing ministry, together with some of the responses to those questions which I find in the Bible.

*What about those who sincerely bring some trouble to the Lord in prayer and ask that it should be removed – only to find that afterwards it seems as bad as ever?*

This is a blockbuster problem. Healings do take place. They can happen against all the odds and can apparently defy explanation. I have seen them. I have written about them. The question is – if healings sometimes happen, why do they not always happen?

I am grateful that the Bible faces this problem head on. We have already seen that in the Old Testament the book of Job does so. In the New Testament St Paul also faces it. For in 2 Corinthians 12.1–10 he tells us about a personal problem, a 'thorn in the flesh', a 'messenger of Satan'. It was clearly a torment to him. It could perhaps have been a painful relationship, for we know he was prone to them. However, the Good News Bible follows the traditional interpretation and paraphrases 'thorn in the flesh' as 'a painful physical ailment'. An eye condition or epilepsy have been suggested. George Bennett wondered whether it might refer to a bad attack of shingles.

Whatever the condition may have been, we are told that even after Paul had prayed three times for healing it remained untouched and Paul was left to discover the mystery of 'power within weakness' (see 2 Corinthians 12.9). It is worth studying the passage in detail. As we do so, important truths emerge.

1  It is essential to note that Paul does *not* regard God as the source of his trouble. He is sure that the affliction comes from Satan. However, it enables him to test one of his fundamental convictions: 'In *all* things God works for good with those who love him' (Romans 8.28).
2  Paul rightly asks for healing. Neither he nor we can understand why healing does not immediately follow,

but though he is not healed *from* his condition, yet gradually he realizes that he is receiving a real degree of healing *within* that condition.

3  His 'thorn in the flesh' provides him with an opportunity for spiritual cleansing and growth. He is able to wield it as a weapon against the sin of pride. He is able to discover new dimensions of the grace of God.

4  He uses it also as an occasion to contemplate some of the more mysterious elements within his Christian experience, for the 'certain Christian man' of whom he speaks in 2 Corinthians 12.2 is almost certainly himself.

5  Note we are *not* told that there was *never* a cure for Paul's trouble. It is a fact of experience that healing can sometimes be inexplicably delayed. There is an illustration of this in the story of my wife, Eira, which I told in Chapter 5 of *Make Me a Channel* (Lawrence, 1996).

6  Certainly Paul did not cease to believe in the ministry of Christian healing – as is indicated by his subsequent healing mission to the people of the island of Malta (Acts 28.1–9).

To summarize: experience (including that of Job and Paul) seems to show that God has both a 'Plan A' and a 'Plan B' in the healing ministry. The overall teaching of Scripture seems clearly to indicate that God's Plan A is for the restoration of total wholeness of body, mind and spirit, for complete healing at every level of our being. Sometimes, however, Plan A can be delayed or even totally blocked. In such cases God's Plan B involves turning a thoroughly undesirable situation unexpectedly to the good. Though outer circumstances do not change, yet those circumstances become the vehicle of a new inner wholeness.

We are not told by Scripture why some people enjoy a Plan A solution to their troubles, whereas others find themselves within a Plan B experience. We must resolutely resist simplistic solutions to this enigma. However, if you should find yourself in a Plan B situation, here is a mysterious and paradoxical scriptural thought. Sometimes God's ultimate purpose can be advanced more profoundly by troubles that are endured and conquered than by troubles that are removed. In fact suffering itself, if offered to God, can become a powerful channel through which Christian healing can flow into the world. It was so in the case of St Paul. And it was supremely so in the case of Jesus.

*How important is forgiveness in the ministry of Christian healing?*

Its importance can hardly be overestimated. It is often an element in the healing of the body (as in Mark 2.1–12). It is always involved in the healing of the spirit. It is at the heart of Christian healing because it is at the heart of the gospel itself.

The Bible is clear about our basic condition. 'All have sinned, and fall short of the glory of God' (Romans 3.23, NIV). 'If we say that we have no sin, we deceive ourselves, and the truth is not in us' (1 John 1.9, AV). The Genesis analysis of the consequence of this still applies. Our sin still separates us from God, from each other and from our own inner integrity.

However, because of the forgiveness which is offered to us in and through Jesus Christ, there can be a healing of the anguish of separation. Forgiveness does no violence to truth. It does not involve pretending that sin is not sin. Forgiving is not forgetting. It is remembering but going on loving just the same – and paying the price of doing so.

This is what Jesus offers you and me from the cross. If we accept that costly forgiveness, we shall find that the relationship with Jesus that ensues has the power to reunite us with

God (Romans 5.11), with our fellow humans (Romans 15.7) and with our inner selves (Romans 8.1–2). St Paul describes this process as that of being 'justified', and I love the rather childish explanation of this word that it means that, although I am a sinner, yet amazingly God is prepared to pay the price of treating me 'just as if I'd never sinned'.

Those who experience the Father's healing forgiveness through Jesus Christ are then called to channel forgiveness into the world. This is not only good for the world, it is good for us too. For in the memorable words of Rabbi Harold Kushner, 'Forgiveness is a favour we do ourselves.' It leaves us happier, healthier, freer people.

For a more detailed treatment of the healing mystery of the cross, see Chapter 8 of *Journey into Mystery*, and for a more detailed treatment of our calling to be channels of healing forgiveness see Chapter 2 of *Make Me a Channel* (Lawrence, 1999; 1996).

## What about the healing of society?

This is a major concern of the Bible. In the Old Testament the prophets thunder against social injustice. The words 'Let justice flow like a stream, and righteousness like a river' (Amos 5.24) could well serve as a motto for all the prophets. The New Testament has a slightly different emphasis and places greater stress on the responsibility of the *individual*. We are taught that we meet Jesus himself in the poor and distressed (Matthew 25.31–46). There are rules for good citizenship (Romans 12.9–13; 1 Peter 2.17). The greatest thing we can do in life is to put God's own love into practical action. Love is the most important of all qualities (1 Corinthians 13). We are called to give it expression at every level of life, particularly when dealing with those who experience hardship and distress (1 John 3.17–18).

*What is the place of individual 'gifts' in the Church's healing ministry?*

Scripture has no doubts that individual gifts exist. Some people have natural aptitudes which can be put at God's disposal. Other gifts come directly from the Holy Spirit, and these include 'gifts of healings' (1 Corinthians 12.9, RV).

However, speaking personally, I am grateful that, so far as I know, I have no special individual gift for the healing ministry. If I had such a gift, I might be tempted to trust *it* – rather than trusting the Lord himself. The scriptural centrepoint of the healing ministry does not lie in the possession of special gifts but in the practice of the presence of Christ. Christians are meant to be so close to Jesus that we can be described in an almost literal way as 'the body of Christ' (1 Corinthians 12.27, AV). Being a Christian involves 'union with Christ' – literally the experience of being 'in Christ' (*en Christo*). This is St Paul's favourite phrase. According to the German scholar Adolf Deissmann, Paul uses this phrase or its equivalent 164 times.

The heart of the Christian healing ministry is union with the healing Christ. We are called to be 'infected' by his healing nature and then to pass on that infection to others. It is a ministry for all Christians, irrespective of whether we may or may not have an individual 'gift'. It is the prime mission of the Church within this sick world. The New Testament stresses that the resources behind this mission must never be underestimated. Indeed the transforming power of union with Christ is such that according to St Paul it can be described as nothing less than 'new creation' (2 Corinthians 5.17, NIV).

*How important are the external phenomena which sometimes accompany Christian healing – heat, light, tingling sensations, 'electric' shocks, falling to the ground, etc.?*

These have a very minor place in Scripture. Some people find them helpful as an indication of God's presence, but there is danger in overemphasizing them. Personally, I know of many occasions when there has been healing, though external phenomena have been totally absent. I also know of occasions when external phenomena have been strongly experienced and yet there has been no subsequent evidence of healing. Again it is important to emphasize that our focus in Christian healing must always be on the presence of the Lord himself rather than on 'signs' of that presence.

## What has the Bible to say about medical treatment?

There is no incompatibility between sound medical practice and a sound Christian healing ministry. We have already seen that some of the Old Testament prophets employed a mixture of spiritual and medical means when they exercised a personal healing ministry. In the New Testament, Timothy is recommended to take a nip of medicinal alcohol when his stomach is out of order (1 Timothy 5.23). Luke, 'the beloved doctor' (see Colossians 4.14), is held in great esteem.

Medical treatment can, in fact, itself be a channel of Christian healing, if it is either offered or received in the name of Jesus and within a consciousness of his presence and healing purpose. For anything at all which reminds us of him and brings us closer to him will thereby have a new dimension and capacity for his work.

## Doctors seem to place an increasing stress on 'preventive medicine'. Is there an equivalent to this within the ministry of Christian healing?

Yes. The Bible stresses the importance of adopting patterns of life which are conducive to health rather than sickness of body, mind and spirit. We are encouraged to fill our minds with positive rather than negative thoughts and to nourish our souls with wholesome spiritual food. 'Whatever is true,' says St Paul, 'whatever is noble, whatever is right, whatever is pure, whatever is lovely, whatever is admirable – if anything is excellent or praiseworthy – think about such things' (Philippians 4.8, NIV).

Just as there is a sense in which at a physical level we are what we eat, so our mental and spiritual health is governed by the nature of those things we take into our minds and spirits. Therefore we do well if we are careful about our choice of books, magazines, videos, TV programmes, etc.

Also just as protective clothing can be important for our bodies, so there is a spiritual equivalent. It is hard to over-estimate the importance of the description of the 'armour of God' in Ephesians 6.11–17.

> Put on all the armour that God gives you, so that you will be able to stand up against the Devil's evil tricks . . . Stand ready, with truth as a belt tight round your waist, with righteousness as your breastplate, and as your shoes the readiness to announce the Good News of peace. At all times carry faith as a shield; for with it you will be able to put out all the burning arrows shot by the Evil One. And accept salvation as a helmet, and the word of God as the sword which the Spirit gives you.

It is well worth pausing for a moment to consider how well or how badly we are armed. For Planet Earth is a place of spiritual warfare and one way or another we will all be caught up in it, whether we know it or not.

Moreover, though it is not generally recognized, the devil offers his own form of 'protective' clothing to those who are wicked enough or foolish enough to put it on. The devil's armour 'protects' us against the influence of health and goodness. John Bunyan writes about it in his important but little-known book *The Holy War*. The helmet is false optimism – the notion that everything will work out well in the end, no matter what we choose and how we live. The breastplate is a hard heart which ensures that judgement cannot frighten us and mercy cannot win us. The sword is a tongue that speaks evil of God, of Jesus, of God's ways and of God's people. The shield is that of unbelief, a total cynicism which calls all values into question, has no care for anything, and is sceptical about everything. In my years as a vicar, I have encountered not a few people wearing this sort of armour, and sometimes doing so with bravado and style. It has always been a desperately sad experience. So are you and I wearing armour? And if so, whose? God's? The devil's? Or even a curious mixture of the two?

### What is meant by a 'healed death'?

We have already considered examples of healed death in Chapter 1 'In the Beginning . . .' Other instances come into my mind as I write.

Agnes, a Christian lady of advanced years who I used to know, announced to her daughter one morning that she did not intend to get up that day, because her time had come and she wanted to die in the comfort of her own bed. The day before she had been perfectly well and she was totally untroubled when she made the announcement. Her daughter scolded her for saying such a thing and sent for the doctor. As the doctor sat by Agnes' bed and took her pulse, to his own surprise he found himself saying, 'Your mother's right. She is dying.' 'Told you so!' said Agnes, and she went on her way into eternity with a smile on her face.

Or how about the story of Roger, which I told in some detail in Chapter 9 of *How to Pray when Life Hurts* (Lawrence, 1993)? Life was not easy for Roger towards the end of his life, even though a remarkable healing extended that life by six years. However, as it came to an end, it would be difficult to find a better example of a truly good and Christian death. One day he sent for me and told me he believed he had only a week to live. He asked me to prepare him a seven-day prayer schedule, so that the week would not be wasted. He planned his funeral in detail and, though the service he designed made no attempt to disguise the pain and the problems he had faced, it was full of faith, joy and gratitude to God for life, thanks to his widowed father who had lovingly cared for him, and an almost excited readiness to embark on the great adventure that lay ahead. Seven days later, having completed his prayer schedule, he died a healed death.

At the heart of such experiences there is the conviction, which has run like a golden thread through Christian history since the days of the New Testament, that the life which Jesus offers to his followers is stronger than death. Early Christians were prepared to die rather than betray their faith, because they were convinced that death could not hold them any more than it could hold their Lord. St Athanasius wrote, 'Man is by nature afraid of death and the dissolution of the body, but the remarkable thing is that when he accepts the faith of the cross, he disregards this natural characteristic and he loses his fear of death.' Around the world Christians still die rather than betray their Lord. The century which has just ended has been characterized, beyond all others, by the witness of Christian martyrs. As this millennium begins, Christian Solidarity Worldwide reports that every three minutes somewhere in the world a new Christian martyr is added to their number.

Their courage shames us, but their faith reminds us that if you and I are serious Christians, if in any real and meaningful way we have put our hand in the hand of Jesus, we are called to know not only that we can walk through this world without fear but that when our time comes to die, Jesus will not wrench his hand from ours. He will hold us firmly and lead us where he himself has already gone – into death and beyond death into the mystery of eternity, where in his presence we will become that which we were created to be. This will be the ultimate healing, the flowering of our being, the greatest and most mysterious of all gifts.

> 'Do not let your hearts be troubled,' said Jesus. 'Believe in God, believe also in me. In my Father's house there are many dwelling-places. If it were not so, would I have told you that I go to prepare a place for you? And if I go and prepare a place for you, I will come again and take you to myself, so that where I am, there you may be also.' (John 14.1–3, NRSV.)

St Paul adds this personal reflection in Philippians 3.10–14 (NRSV):

> I want to know Christ and the power of his resurrection and the sharing of his sufferings by becoming like him in his death . . . Not that I have already obtained this or have already reached the goal; but I press on to make it my own . . . Beloved, I do not consider that I have made it my own; but this one thing I do: forgetting what lies behind and straining forward to what lies ahead, I press on towards the goal for the prize of the heavenly call of God in Christ Jesus.

Of course, the death of loved ones can bring great sadness to those who are left behind, but for those who have the privilege of actually experiencing 'healed death' there is no sadness. St Paul speaks of it in terms of 'victory' (1 Corinthians 15.54) and 'gain' (Philippians 1.21). He tells us plainly that, if we allow Christ to heal our attitude to death, we shall find ourselves contemplating our own death without fear. Indeed we shall contemplate it with hope and optimism, and in the positive expectation that the best is yet to be.

*Finally, what of human history as a whole? How will it all end?*

There are many hints about the answer to this question throughout the Gospels and the Epistles, but it is the book of Revelation that sets its face to consider the end of human history as we know it. As it does so we become aware of a strange return to the atmosphere of the very earliest part of the Bible. For the book of Revelation is not a literal exposé of the events at the end of the world any more than Genesis is a literal record of our historical origins. Once again we find ourselves involved in another drama which is relevant to every age – and certainly to our own.

The author begins with messages for seven contemporary churches. He stresses the theme which is at the heart of the whole of the New Testament, that for Christians nothing is more important than the presence of the living Christ in our midst. 'Listen,' says Jesus, 'I stand at the door and knock; if anyone hears my voice and opens the door, I will come into his house and eat with him, and he will eat with me. To those who win the victory I will give the right to sit beside me on my throne, just as I have been victorious and now sit by my Father on his throne' (Revelation 3.20–21).

He then shares a vision – he calls it 'an open door in heaven' (Revelation 4.1) – not so that we can know the dates, times and details of the last things, for that was knowledge which was not even given to Jesus (Mark 13.32), but so that here and now we may be guided, encouraged and healed by those truths which are greater than time itself. Here are some of them:

1  There is a mystery of evil, just as there is a mystery of

goodness. Both are beyond the range of human understanding. We need a language of signs and symbols in
order to approach either of them, and signs and symbols
are to be found in plenty within this final book of
Scripture.

2  Evil has power to create havoc – even greater havoc than
the world has yet seen – for the origins are to be found
not only within the misuse of the free will of fallen
humankind but within a strange and baleful realm of
fallen 'principalities and powers'.

3  However, evil will *not* be allowed to have the last word.
Jesus will not only have the last word, he will *be* the last
word. Even now he is at work, healing hurts and bringing
good out of evil, wherever he is given any sort of access.
But ultimately this work will be cosmic and complete.
Healing will prevail. All will know that goodness is
stronger than evil, healing stronger than destruction.

4  This conviction has the power to encourage and strength-
en the forces of goodness here and now. For all the chaos
and horror which evil can generate, it has suffered a
death blow through the life, death and resurrection of
Jesus. Evil is like a headless chicken, still dashing around
a farmyard, yet destined to collapse. Christians are called
not only to look forward to the final victory, but also
mysteriously to live within it even now. We are to pray
both 'thy kingdom come' and 'thine *is* the kingdom'.

5  Consequently, just as Christians should live a life which
is free from the fear of death at a personal level, so we
are called to experience a freedom from fear as we contemplate the worldwide and cosmic scene. In the words
of Mother Julian, 'All shall be well, and all shall be
well, and all manner of things shall be well' – a conviction born not out of wishful thinking but as a logical
consequence of belief in God.

6 Scripture makes it clear that no one will be forced to accept union with God. Even though he is the source and goal of life, God will continue to allow the negative miracle of the misuse of free will with all its self-destructive implications. The possibility of hell is the inexorable consequence of the reality of free will. However, because of the redemptive work of Jesus, the way into the Father's presence lies open before us. For those who will have it, union with God can and will be a living and eternal reality.

7 So it is that after many pages which set out the dreadful consequences for any who insist on their right to embrace the serpent's temptation to 'be like God' and who choose to brandish the banner of self-centred pride in the face of the Creator to the very end, the book of Revelation concludes by turning from the darkness and facing the eternal light. As we have leafed our way through the pages of the Bible, we find that it has involved a change of leaves in more than one sense. For the Bible begins with the 'leaves of shame' with which Adam and Eve pathetically tried to cover their nakedness and conceal their disobedience, but it ends with 'leaves of healing', freely available within the city of God. 'The angel also showed me the river of the water of life, sparkling like crystal, and coming from the throne of God and of the Lamb and flowing down the middle of the city's street. On each side of the river was the tree of life, which bears fruit twelve times a year, once each month; and its leaves are for the healing of the nations' (Revelation 22.1–2).

These words take me back to an occasion on Monday 9 March 1981, when I was privileged to lead an evening on the theme of Christian healing in that city in Northern

Ireland which cannot be named. For if it is called Londonderry, the Republicans are affronted, and if it is called Derry, the Loyalists are equally offended. The evening started with a public meeting and ended with a late-night healing service in the church of St Peter, Heathfield. St Peter's has a lovely stained glass window depicting the river of life from the book of Revelation. Into its current have fallen leaves from the tree of life, the leaves of healing. I remember speaking about its powerful symbolism. It seemed a remote possibility in those terror-torn days and even as I write these words today the tug of war continues between healing and hurting, between hatred and reconciliation, and yet as I saw Roman Catholic and Protestant clergy and people sitting together in the congregation, I knew that in a sense the vision had already started to become a reality and together we claimed it in faith.

As we read our Bibles from Genesis to Revelation, we will find ourselves challenged to make similar claims in faith. May God help us and guide us as we meet that challenge. May we find, each one of us, the healing which is available to us in the Bible. And, if we find it, God grant we may not keep it to ourselves.

For the Scriptures tell the story of a people who are offered healing in order that they themselves may become a channel of healing, and you and I are invited to become such people too, people of the healing Book, people of the healing Christ, people whose destiny is a heavenly city where healing will be complete and the love, life and glory of God will be all in all.

# EPILOGUE
## *Your Personal Bible Plan*

The final part of this book is very short – but it is dispro-
portionately important. If you take it seriously, it will
require more of your time and attention than everything
that has gone before. For the Bible is not just a healing
book in a general way. It is also able to bring healing in a
very personal way to each one of us. Whatever our own
specific area of need may be, our healing God can meet us
there and minister to us through the Bible.

These final pages contain a sequence of passages from
Scripture for your consideration. Some of them have already
appeared earlier in this book. Some have not. They all have
a potential for healing. But we have to make them our own
before this healing potential becomes a personal reality.

The study method which I want to offer you will require
a full year if you are to implement it. My suggestion is that
every week you take a Bible passage and each day you
read it carefully and unhurriedly, and then allow yourself
to be still before it for some minutes, gently waiting to see if
the text will come to life for you. The odds are that on the
first day absolutely nothing will happen, and the next day,
if the same procedure is followed, nothing may happen
again. But on the third and fourth day tiny gleaming lights
may well begin to shine into your spirit: new glimmerings
of understanding, new pointers for living, new resources

for your inner life. These lights will shine more brightly as the week continues, and by the time it comes to an end, the text could well be ablaze with light and truth and healing.

The Holy Spirit will not only have led you into truth in a general way but also will have helped you to see what is true for *you*. For it is God's way to personalize his truth, and when we perceive God's personalized truth, its effect will be to set us free – free to know ourselves, free to know him, and free to know his purpose for us. With that truth and that freedom there come hope and healing.

Every human being is unique and every week of personalized Bible study can have a unique yield. Some readers will go deeper than others. Some will see further than others. It does not matter. In the words of Pope Gregory the Great, 'The Bible is like a wide river in which lambs may splash in the shallows and elephants may swim to their hearts' content.' What matters is that whether we are natural splashers or swimmers, we approach Scripture at our own level and wait upon God, whose will it is to communicate with us and who will use the words of the Bible for that purpose, if we give him the mental and spiritual space to do so.

So how are *you* to find hope and healing through the Bible? Providing you take this long-term exercise seriously, then you are about to find out the answer. Enjoy the hunt. Have a good Bible probe. And may the healing power of the Holy Spirit be in you.

**Week one. Genesis 1.1—2.4.** We are here for a reason.

**Week two. Genesis 2.4b–25.** We are meant to be one with God, one with each other and one with our own inner selves.

**Week three. Genesis 3.** Everything goes wrong when self is put at the centre of life.

**Week four. Genesis 4.1–15.** Sin is terrible and destructive, but sinners are still precious to God.

**Week five. Genesis 6 and 7.** 'The wages of sin is death' . . .

**Week six. Genesis 8.1—9.17. . . .** but God's will is for restoration and life.

**Week seven. Genesis 11.1–9; 12.1–3.** Without God there is chaos, but with God there is always hope.

**Week eight. Exodus 3.1–10.** We encounter God at unexpected times.

**Week nine. Exodus 4.1–15.** We are often reluctant to serve God, but when he calls us he also empowers us.

**Week ten. Exodus 14.5–31.** God delivers those who put their trust in him.

**Week eleven. Exodus 15.22–26.** God is revealed as 'the Lord who heals'.

**Week twelve. Exodus 20.1–21.** The Ten Commandments.

**Week thirteen. Numbers 21.4–9.** A strange healing.

**Week fourteen. Deuteronomy 30.15–20.** A matter of life and death.

**Week fifteen. Joshua 1.1–9.** A commission and a promise.

**Week sixteen. 1 Samuel 16.1–13.** God's choices are sometimes surprising.

**Week seventeen. 1 Samuel 17.1–50.** David and Goliath.

**Week eighteen. 2 Samuel 11.1—12.13.** King David's sin. King David's repentance.

**Week nineteen. 1 Kings 3.** The wisdom of Solomon.

**Week twenty. 2 Kings 5.1–14.** The healing of Naaman.

**Week twenty-one. 2 Chronicles 7.** The temple of God.

**Week twenty-two. Job 19.13–27.** Job holds on to his faith in spite of his suffering.

**Week twenty-three. Psalm 23.** 'The Lord is my shepherd.'

**Week twenty-four. Psalm 46.** A psalm of trust.

**Week twenty-five. Psalm 103.** A psalm of praise.

**Week twenty-six. Proverbs 3.1–7; 4.20–27.** Healing wisdom.

**Week twenty-seven. Isaiah 11.1–9.** The coming kingdom.

**Week twenty-eight.** Isaiah 40. Words of hope.

**Week twenty-nine.** Isaiah 53. God's Messiah will be required to suffer for us.

**Week thirty.** Jeremiah 17.5–14. A prophet writes of healing.

**Week thirty-one.** Ezekiel 37.1–14. Life that is stronger than death.

**Week thirty-two.** Luke 4.16–30. Jesus claims the role of Messiah.

**Week thirty-three.** Luke 5.1–26. Jesus calls the first disciples and exercises a healing ministry.

**Week thirty-four.** Luke 8.26–56. His healing ministry continues.

**Week thirty-five.** Luke 9.1–6; 10.1–20. He shares the healing ministry with his followers.

**Week thirty-six.** Luke 11.1–13. Jesus teaches about prayer and promises the Holy Spirit.

**Week thirty-seven.** Luke 15.11–32. It is never too late to turn to God.

**Week thirty-eight.** Luke 23. Jesus dies on the cross for us.

**Week thirty-nine.** Luke 24. Jesus rises from the dead and ascends into heaven.

**Week forty.** John 1.1–18. Jesus was and is involved in the creation of life.

**Week forty-one.** John 3.1–17. Jesus offers new birth.

**Week forty-two.** John 4.1—5.18. Jesus, the vulnerable healer, speaks words of power.

**Week forty-three.** John 6.1–40. Jesus feeds the 5,000 and proclaims himself the bread of life.

**Week forty-four.** John 10.1–16. Jesus, the good shepherd.

**Week forty-five.** John 14.1–14. Jesus, our way to the Father.

**Week forty-six.** Acts 3.1–16. The early Church in healing action.

**Week forty-seven. Romans 8.1–17.** Life in the Holy Spirit.

**Week forty-eight. 2 Corinthians 12.1–10.** Visions and problems.

**Week forty-nine. Ephesians 6.10–17.** The armour of God.

**Week fifty. Philippians 4.4–7.** Joy, peace and positive thinking.

**Week fifty-one. 1 John 2.7–17.** Love will conquer everything.

**Week fifty-two. Revelation 3.20–21; 22.1–5.** Jesus is the heart of Christian life today and will be the heart of God's eternal kingdom, where God will banish all darkness and evil and healing will be complete.

# References and Further Reading

Bennett, George (1970) *Miracle at Crowhurst*, Arthur James.

Gordon, Ernest (1963) *Miracle on the River Kwai*, Collins.

Lawrence, Roy (1993) *How to Pray when Life Hurts*, Scripture Union.

Lawrence, Roy (1996) *Make Me a Channel*, Scripture Union.

Lawrence, Roy (1997) *Christ with Us*, Scripture Union.

Lawrence, Roy (1998) *The Practice of Christian Healing*, SPCK.

Lawrence, Roy (1999) *Journey into Mystery*, SPCK.

Lemon, Fred (1977) *Breakout*, Marshall, Morgan & Scott.